The Intersection of Material and Poetic Economy

AF773550

North American Studies
in 19th-Century German Literature

Jeffrey L. Sammons
General Editor

Vol. 42

PETER LANG
Oxford • Bern • Berlin • Bruxelles • Frankfurt am Main • New York • Wien

Anna H. Helm

The Intersection of Material and Poetic Economy

Gustav Freytag's Soll und Haben *and Adalbert Stifter's* Der Nachsommer

PETER LANG
Oxford • Bern • Berlin • Bruxelles • Frankfurt am Main • New York • Wien

Bibliographic information published by Die Deutsche Bibliothek
Die Deutsche Bibliothek lists this publication in the Deutsche Nationalbibliografie; detailed bibliographic data is available on the Internet at ‹http://dnb.ddb.de›.

A catalogue record for this book is available from The British Library.

Library of Congress Cataloging-in-Publication Data:

Helm, Anna, 1967-
The intersection of material and poetic economy : Gustav Freytag‘s Soll und Haben and Adalbert Stifter‘s Der Nachsommer / Anna Helm.
p. cm. -- (North American studies in nineteenth-century German literature ; 42)
Includes bibliographical references and index.
ISBN 978-3-03911-084-1 (alk. paper)
1. Freytag, Gustav, 1816-1895. Soll und Haben. 2. Stifter, Adalbert, 1805-1868. Nachsommer. 3. Money in literature. 4. Economics in literature. 5. Aesthetics in literature. 6. Economics and literature--Germany--History--19th century. I. Title.
PT1873.S63H46 2009
833‘.8--dc22
2009010216

ISSN 0891-4095
ISBN 978-3-03911-084-1

© Peter Lang AG, International Academic Publishers, Bern 2009
Hochfeldstrasse 32, Postfach 746, CH-3000 Bern 9, Switzerland
info@peterlang.com, www.peterlang.com, www.peterlang.net

All rights reserved.
All parts of this publication are protected by copyright.
Any utilisation outside the strict limits of the copyright law, without the permission of the publisher, is forbidden and liable to prosecution. This applies in particular to reproductions, translations, microfilming, and storage and processing in electronic retrieval systems.

Printed in Germany

Contents

Acknowledgements 7

Introduction
The Discourse of Money in Literature 9

Part One – *Soll und Haben*: The Pursuit of Bourgeois Material and Poetic Wealth

Introduction 27
Textualization through Familial and Financial Ties 32
Poesy and Commodity Exchange 43
Industrial Production and Labor 49
Consumption, Wealth, and Pleasure 57
Representation, Credit, and Credibility 62
Bookkeeping and the Fair Price 69
The Feminine Domain 76
The Life and Death of Money 83
The *Geheimbuch* and Poetic Realism 87
Conclusion 93

Part Two – *Der Nachsommer*: The Economy of Aesthetics

Introduction 97
The Father's House and Aesthetic Education 99
Money, Consumption, and the Capitalist Economy 107
Production, Agriculture, and Interaction with Nature 113
The Accumulation of Wealth and Collecting 120
The Fair Price and the Silence of the Market 127
Naming, Signification, and the Creation of Meaning 131

Work, Usefulness, and the Productive Use of Time 136
The Economy of Realism 143
Inheritance and the Sublimation of the Fathers 153
Conclusion 159

Conclusion 163

Bibliography 169
Index 179

Acknowledgements

I dedicate this book to my sons: Sixten, whose endless struggles and survivor's spirit inspire me and remind me of what is important in life; Gustav, whose creativity and energy amaze and exhaust me; and Ludvig, whose blissful smile and determined expressions of baby willpower give me comfort and hope.

A number of individuals have inspired and supported this project. Initially, Dr Simon Richter encouraged me to combine my interests in business and literature by focusing on the intersection of economics and aesthetics in literature. These studies were then continued under Dr Peter Pfeiffer at Georgetown University, who patiently guided me through the intellectual process of writing my dissertation on the topic. I am immensely grateful for his insightful and thought-provoking suggestions and advice, and for serving as my mentor. I also thank my editor, Professor Jeffrey Sammons, for providing me with the opportunity to publish this book. His expertise and genuine interest in this project impressed me and encouraged me to pursue and complete it.

I would also like to express my gratitude to my colleagues in the International Business Department and the Center for International Business Education and Research (GW-CIBER) at the George Washington University for the opportunity to further pursue my interdisciplinary visions and scholarly work in such a wonderfully supportive and inspiring environment. I owe special thanks to Afrora, my assistant, from whose talent and conscientiousness this project tremendously benefited.

Finally, I would like to express my gratitude to my friends and family for reserving a space for me in their lives – having that space and being able to count on them enabled me to exceed my own, limited capacity! I would especially like to acknowledge and thank my parents who have unconditionally supported me in every imaginable way, and who have served as role models, both on a personal and professional level. With the publication of this book, I would also like to honor my amazing grandmother, Farmor Majken, whose positive, spirited nature has given me strength and confidence. Last, but not least, thank you to my husband Robert, my love, for standing by me through the years.

Introduction
The Discourse of Money in Literature

> Money does not occur in nature, and no version or analog of it exists among any other members of the animal kingdom. Money, like language, is uniquely human. Money constituted a new way of thinking and acting that changed the world immediately. Only now, after nearly three thousand years, is the full power of money becoming apparent in human affairs, as it supplants or dominates many of the traditional social bonds based on family, tribe, community, and nation (Weatherford, 27).

Money defines many aspects of human existence, such as the exchange of goods and the ways in which we represent value. Money has a direct influence on social behavior because it promotes a monetarization of value by equating any kind of product, tangible or intangible, to a common denominator. In a money economy, all goods and services can be expressed using this common denominator, money. The metaphorical character of money – the fact that it always stands for something else – provides money with the ability to implement new structures of thought.

The processes of signification changed in society when money was elevated from being just one commodity among many to an exclusive position as the measure of all things. Modern money[1] has an

1 One important attribute of modern money is that is serves as the *exclusive* means of exchange. Jack Weatherford (1997) points out that the Aztecs used cacao beans for money. In some ways their cacao beans had many of modern money's attributes (for example, criminals would "counterfeit" cacao beans by emptying their husks and replacing the contents with mud), but cacao bean money was not the general equivalent of modern money because it merely served as a way to "calculate value and to round out the exchange, but it did not serve as the exclusive means of exchange" (19). The dominant principle of this "commodity money" society was still barter trade. In addition, as Jochen Hörisch (2000) indicates, a distinguishing factor of modern money is that it is guaranteed by the leadership of the society in which it is being circulated: "A ruler acquires credit for himself not least of all by creating and authorizing a

infinite capacity to represent, and ultimately subsume, all other things. Its move from facilitator in the process of exchange to holder of endless possibility had a destabilizing effect because accurate representation was no longer possible. The distinction between signifier and signified was compromised. Furthermore, subsequent shifts in money form (the physical shape of money itself, such as coins made of precious metals and alloys, paper money, and electronic money) have had a fundamental impact on human life, inspiring new ideas in the realms of literary and philosophical thought. Literary critics such as Marc Shell, Richard T. Gray, Jochen Hörisch, and John Vernon have focused on the connection between economic thought and literature.

In an economy based on the exchange of gold coins for products and services there is a direct correlation between the purchasing power of the coin and the value of its metallic substance; the inscription on gold coins precisely represents the value of the metal from which they are made. The idea of a linkage between the substance of money and its inscribed value was reinforced by the gold standard, in which a central bank was required to keep a sufficient supply of gold to cover the value of government promissory notes. Over time, this strict relationship between symbol and substance in gold coins was diffused by the introduction of other forms of money that strayed from a direct correlation of value, such as coins made of alloy, and, eventually, paper and electronic money. These alternative and more modern money forms, to a greater or lesser extent, represent value without being "guaranteed" by the substance from which they are made.

---

valid currency. The head lends the number on the other side authority and validity […]" At the same time "the number on the coin acquires validity and recognition not least of all through the authority of the one who issues it […]" (15). Hörisch takes this idea further by contending that there is a circular relationship between heads and tails of coins, and that both sides of the coin have authority to the extent that they become one in the coin: "This means, however, that heads and tails obtain their authority, their cover and their validity from a third entity, into which they are synthesized: from the coin whose sides they are […]" (15).

Changes in money form have brought about debates concerning the nature of language[2] and representation within the economy. The substance of the debates revolved around the question of whether it was acceptable to abandon what was considered "real money" with a commodity value, such as gold, for money that merely represented value, and in that sense was not "real".[3] These debates on monetary representation and the metaphoric language they generated were picked up in other discourses in which issues such as value, substance, and representation played a significant role. "Economic" patterns of

2 The debate concerning the structural similarities between language and money has a long history. To give an example, Klaus Riegel (1979) compares monetary and linguistic systems by building on the changes in money form over time. His discussion begins with a comparison of the barter system with proto-language, stating that both, despite their relative simplicity, rely on basic rules (61). Further, Riegel compares the coinage system to token language (a system which has ways of expressing temporal and spatial properties) (64). The significance of the coinage system was its ability to accommodate delayed and sequential exchanges and multiple distributions (63). The last set of systems in Riegel's comparison is that of the debenture system and interaction language. Relevant here is that he distinguishes the debenture system from the paper money form, stating that it would be "misleading to think about paper money only in terms of the common bills issued by national banks" (66). Instead, he proposes the inclusion of bonds issued and guaranteed by national governments, as well as by corporations. The introduction of different forms of paper money allowed the economy to expand and ultimately to reflect the "sum total of activities in which a whole nation, an industrial complex, or lastly, a single individual was, is, or was to be engaged" (67). Riegel concludes that neither the barter nor the coinage systems are appropriate to use in the comparison with language: "An adequate understanding of language can be achieved only through comparisons with the debenture system which is based upon matrices of transactions rather than upon classes of fixed elements" (67).

3 A good example of the debate about coined and paper money is the American political discourse from 1825 to 1875. The advocates of paper money – the paper money men – were set against the advocates of gold – the gold bugs – in a debate on monetary and aesthetic symbolization, i.e., the relationship between the substantial thing and its sign. Marc Shell (1982) has incorporated this debate into a chapter on Poe's *The Gold Bug* (5–23).

thought, such as money metaphors, tropes, and symbols, have claimed their place in intellectual discourse and literature.[4]

Marc Shell, for example, has made economic thought a central tenet of his style of literary interpretation. In *The Economy of Literature* (1978), Shell focuses on the relationship between economic and verbal representation. Among other things, he investigates why coinage, tyranny, and philosophy developed in the same time and place. Another important topic in this book is the semiology of coins as material media of exchange and as symbols or works of literature. In *Money, Language, and Thought* (1982), Shell interprets literary and philosophical works by exploring the ways in which money speaks in and through their discourse. He focuses on topics such as dispensation, usury, and hypothesizing which, in his words, are "telling intellectual procedures through which economic form expresses itself in language" (Shell 1982, 181).

In his interpretations of literary and philosophical texts, Shell explores issues of symbolization relating to the realm of the economy. In the conclusion of his book *The Economy of Literature*, Shell states that the work "seeks to understand dialectically the relationship between thought and matter by looking from the formal similarities between linguistic and economic symbolization and production to the political economy as a whole" (Shell 1978, 152).

In his approach to literature, Shell draws on a wealth of economic and philosophical traditions. He does not simply suggest that a relationship between money, language, and thought exists but rather establishes the *necessity* of such a relationship. Shell emphasizes the

4 Richard T. Gray (1996), for example, has used an economic perspective in his interpretations of German bourgeois literature: "One of the hypotheses that my essays pursue is that the economic conflict between use-value, or intrinsic worth, and exchange-value, or extrinsic worth defined in the differential system of exchange, parallels not only the dialectic struggle constitutive of bourgeois (self)-divided subjectivity, but likewise the structural tensions inherent in the bourgeois work of art" (16). In his interpretations, Gray focuses on a close reading of the canonized, literary texts of his choice, but draws conclusions that have social-political implications. One of his contentions is that the middle class authors were struggling more against bourgeois economic practices than against an oppressor external to their own class (2).

tropic interaction between economic and linguistic symbolization and production: "Literary works are composed of small tropic exchanges or metaphors, some of which can be analyzed in terms of signified economic content and all of which can be analyzed in terms of economic form" (7). The primary goal of literary criticism, according to Shell, is understanding the connection between literary exchange (such as the connections between the smallest verbal metaphors and the largest tropes) and the exchanges that constitute the political economy.

Shell's analysis of tropic interaction in literary discourse can be exemplified by his interpretation of Goethe's *Faust*, which focuses on how the concept of "translation" (*Übertragung*) has both a linguistic (as relating to meaning) and an economic (as relating to property) component in the drama. One aspect of translation that Shell discusses relates to paper money and its inflationary tendencies. Shell draws the conclusion that there are strong commonalities between the "mentality" of paper money, idealist philosophy, and Mephistopheles' linguistic doctrine which disassociates words and concepts (1982, 99–111). Mephistopheles is the proponent of what Shell calls both a monetary and linguistic immaterialism (104).

Shell's work exposes the "money of the mind" which exists, sometimes openly, sometimes latently, in any text. The participation of economic form in literature and philosophy is defined by the tropic interaction between economic and linguistic symbolization and production, and not by content. "A formal money of the mind informs all discourse and is as unaffected by whether or not the thematic content of a particular work includes money as by whether or not the material content of the ink in which the work may be inscribed includes gold" (4). Shell rejects critical approaches to literature that focus exclusively on economic content because "such studies fail to consider the formal similarities between metaphorization (which characterizes all language and literature) and economic representation and exchange" (1978, 3).

Shell's work is heavily focused on philosophical discourse. He mostly discusses philosophical concepts as pertaining to the words and structures of thought that they have borrowed from the realm of economics. Shell also uses a specific linguistic analysis that draws on the common heritage of certain words that connote both economic concepts and philosophical and linguistic thought such as *seme*, which in Greek means both "coin" and "word" (1982, 2). Due to Shell's pronounced concentration on philosophical discourse and reliance on this type of linguistic analysis, his approach is only partially applicable to my interpretation of *Soll und Haben* and *Der Nachsommer*. My analysis has no direct link to philosophical texts. Instead, my approach constitutes above all a close reading of the primary texts and offers an interpretation in light of the secondary literature on realist representation. However, Shell's contention that an analysis of economic form in literature is universally applicable because literary theory necessarily deals with concepts such as verbal value and therefore cannot avoid economic and political problems is convincing (1978, 6). It was Shell's insistence on the necessity of these connections between money, language and thought that piqued my interest in a comparison between a novel that focuses on the economic (*Soll und Haben*) and a novel that distances itself from it (*Der Nachsommer*).

In his studies of nineteenth Century British literature John Vernon points out that the realistic novel is an outcome of the changes in the "art of representation" that took place in all spheres of life, including art, politics, economics, and religion, during this time. Vernon connects these changes in modes of representation with changes in money form:

> The shift from metal currency to paper money indicates a more general shift that submitted immediate reality to a kind of semantic coding; and the realistic novel was part of this shift. As money was becoming more fictional, fiction was becoming not only more profitable, not merely more concerned with economic themes, but also more mediated, more representational, more omniscient – in a word, more realistic [...] (Vernon, 17–18).

Further, Vernon claims that "the failure of money, the fact that paper money is money, but at the same time the absence of money, parallels in the realistic novel the failure of mimesis, which can never be a pure, homogeneous extension of its world" (19). This notion is important and has served as a guiding principle in my own interpretation.

In the two novels that I will interpret, *Der Nachsommer* by Adalbert Stifter and *Soll und Haben* by Gustav Freytag, the narrative revolves around the problem of representing reality in art, literature, and finance. While Stifter focuses his attention on the aesthetic aspects of private life, Freytag poeticizes the life of the bourgeois merchant in the public economy. The two works have in common the thematization and integration into their "poetic plots" of certain phenomena that accompanied industrialization, such as the concept of credit, consumption, and financial speculation. These thematic realms are locations in the novels at which economic and aesthetic representation coincide and mutually inform each other.

Vernon emphasizes the importance of some of these concepts by pointing out that the Industrial Revolution was not the beginning of capitalism, but rather the "final climactic stage of a long process in which its characteristic devices and apparatus – credit, speculation, bills of exchange, banks, investment capital – evolved largely out of international trade" (29). The shift to paper money was an ongoing process with roots going back several hundred years. The widespread acceptance of paper money, however, was unique to the nineteenth century. Money in the nineteenth century was qualitatively different from money in previous ages because, as many other critics have also noted, it was symbolic money – paper, paper inscribed with text.[5]

Constant change and insecurity were exacerbated by evolving ideas concerning money and wealth. Vernon presents his finding that with the changes brought about by the Industrial Revolution, wealth gradually came to be thought of as an active agent, a power.[6] It

5 Here again is the foundation of Shell's (1978 and 1982) critical discourse on literature and philosophy ("electrum" to electricity), and Hörisch's (2000) focus on the compromised materiality of paper money: "Monitor-money is quite plausibly the logical conclusion of the development from concrete value via minted gold and assignats to the check and from signed paper on into the sphere of the fully immaterial" (65).

6 This new force needs to be compared to the "old" habits of thought, i.e., that the only real money was gold and that the only stable and secure form of wealth was land. According to Vernon (1984), the transition to paper money and the new concept of wealth was a long-drawn-out process that extended back to the previous century (33).

became a means of expansion and increase, of augmentation, amplification, and multiplication.[7] Paper money especially gave rise to a more volatile and unpredictable conception of wealth. As a literary example of the economic implications of changes in money form, Vernon establishes a connection to literary realism by discussing different literary types and their relationship to money, specifically the miser's connection to gold and the spendthrift's to paper money.[8] The miser seeks a shield from change, increase, expansion, the unknown, and the future by accumulating wealth. The spendthrift, on the other hand, gets social energy and companionship by spending money. Money for spendthrifts is not real; it is merely the paper image of money (36–7). This is because "gold tends to stay in one place, in contrast to paper, which is inclined to circulate. Gold is hoarded, paper spent, gold is stable and paper unstable, gold attracts misers and paper spendthrifts" (35). The connection of gold coins to stability and paper money to instability is a prominent theme also in *Soll und Haben* that informs the greater issue of representation in the novel.

It is precisely these types of intersections of the material and poetic economies that are of interest in my investigation of *Soll und Haben* and *Der Nachsommer*: how money issues are related to the problematization of the limitations of realist representation as presented in these two literary works, as well as the overlapping modes in

7 Gordon Craig (1982) points out that also in Germany, in "the new integrated capitalistic society, money possessed a power and a seductive attractiveness that it had not possessed for the masses of society during most of human history. It thus assumed palpably magical qualities" (108).

8 In his chapter entitled "The Gold Standard and the Logic of Naturalism" Walter Benn Michaels (1987) explores the miser's relationship to money. He concludes that the miser is not really interested in the money itself but instead in its indefinite potentialities, i.e., the power to buy, even though the miser refuses to exercise that power. The miser "exhibits the psychological law that the potential has often a greater influence over our mind than the actual" (140). Michaels traces the origin of these ideas to Georg Simmel and his *Philosophie des Geldes* (1900). Gordon Craig (1982) emphasizes money's ability to transform itself into any object of desire. He quotes Schopenhauer, saying that the focus on and love for money is a natural one because: "Money alone is the absolute property, because it satisfies not merely one need *in concreto*, but need as such *in abstracto*" (108).

which they deal with the formal aspects of representation in literature and economics.[9] I have coined the word "economopoetics" in order better to be able to facilitate the discussion of the intersections of the material and poetic economies in the two novels. The concept refers to the informative connections between economic and aesthetic structures in literary discourse and, more specifically in the case of my interpretation of *Der Nachsommer* and *Soll und Haben*, to the symbiotic[10] relationship between money form and representational considerations as pertaining to Poetic Realism.

There is a rich tradition among philosophers and literary critics of exploring the connection between economic and literary discourse. Again, Marc Shell relates what he calls the development from "electrum to electricity," i.e., from coins to electronic money, to forms of representation and symbolization in literature and philosophy. Shell insists that this relationship is universal and therefore applicable to the literary and philosophical thought of all times. John Vernon (1984) also views the relationship between money and literature as essential in his exploration of British literature. However, he contends that economic approaches to literary scholarship are more productive for specific literary periods such as, for example, nineteenth century realism. Based on French literary tradition, Jean-Joseph Goux has developed a similar thesis concerning the relationship between money and literature in which he focuses on the idea of money as the "general equivalent," and how the concept of the general equivalent manifests itself in literature.[11]

9 Russell Berman (1986) points out that the descriptive nature of post-1848 writing coincides with a focus on commodities in the real world. Realist literature is concerned with the "new wealth of commodities which it tries to organize and reproduce within the framework of literary communication: an equal exchange of the images of commodities" (60). Organizing and reproducing products and artifacts are important in both the novels, *Soll und Haben* and *Der Nachsommer*. In both texts these activities take place in the representational act of writing, as well as in the aesthetic/economic realms of the novels and therefore are important to my analysis of the works.

10 I am using the word symbiotic to express how the economic and poetic mutually rely on each other in these two works.

11 As Jochen Hörisch (2000) has pointed out, the cultural contexts of Britain and France are quite different in their relation to money, which explains Vernon's

Drawing on this research, my thesis is that the move to a more abstract and symbolic representation in the money economy has had significant impact specifically on the literary discourse of the nineteenth century, which was the zenith of change in money form. I place myself in a rich tradition of philosophers and literary critics who have explored economic thought in literary and philosophical discourse.

I suggest that the exploration of the traces of economic structures in literature contributes to the discourse on literary tendencies and movements by adding what I call an "economopoetic" dimension. I employ this concept on three levels in my literary interpretation. First, there is the content level which includes economic and business related topics with simultaneous poetic implications. This level also includes economic language, for example metaphors. The second level pertains to representational issues, and in particular, to the process of exchange. This level focuses on the structural similarities between the way in which money mediates in the process of commodity exchange and the way in which *Schrift* mediates in the exchange between reality and literary text. The third level relates to economopoetics as a literary strategy. This is really an economopoetic representational model whereby the author makes explicit connections between the material and poetic economy. The way in which Gustav Freytag poeticizes the bourgeois economy in *Soll und Haben* is an example of economopoetics as a literary strategy. The three levels of economopoetics often interact with each other but this is not necessary.

In many cases, economopoetics is a helpful component in shaping a better comprehension of issues of representation, exchange between text and reality, and the creation of meaning between reader and text. My investigation will focus on the economopoetics of two novels within the German-speaking tradition: Gustav Freytag's *Soll und Haben* (1855) and Adalbert Stifter's *Der Nachsommer* (1857). This exploration of economopoetics is a tool to develop interpretations that comment on fundamental issues of literary realism pertaining to

---

and Goux's slightly diverging viewpoints: "[...] Anglo-Saxon literature has tried to compensate for the insufficient realism of paper money with its realism; French literature, on the other hand, repeatedly points to the illusory quality of the gold standard" (72).

the two novels. The purpose of my inquiry is to explore the three economopoetic levels in an actual textual analysis and to clarify how it can function as a tool in literary interpretations.

In *Soll und Haben* and *Der Nachsommer* the viability of realist representation, the process of mimesis in general, and the nature of language and *Schriftlichkeit* are scrutinized through themes and motifs that are inherent to the sphere of the material economy. Specifically, it is my conviction that Freytag and Stifter, in spite of their insistence on realist representation, to some degree question and at times even undermine their own realism. This aesthetic tension is decipherable from the way in which economic principles of the money economy are evoked semantically in the two novels. Literary realism, then, allows some degree of idealism, i.e., that it describes not what is but what should be. In a sense, it becomes a promise just as paper money is a promise.

In choosing Freytag's *Soll und Haben* and Stifter's *Der Nachsommer* I considered numerous criteria. Marc Shell's argument that all literary works speak economics led me to compare a novel that explicitly focuses on business and economics (*Soll und Haben*) and a novel that distances itself from it (*Der Nachsommer*). Already the title *Soll und Haben* implies the importance of economic themes and the existence of an organizing economic principle that allows for better "readability" of economic activities and representations. The novel directly and overtly employs the economic discourse of its time. In contrast, *Der Nachsommer* distances itself from that very discourse. In this discrepancy between the two novels lies the main justification of my choice of texts: I will show that even a novel like *Der Nachsommer* that clearly wants to liberate itself from "money talk" is mired in it as it develops a very different kind of aesthetics.

In addition, there are many parallel developments in the themes of the two novels. Both novels are *Bildungsromane* in which the educational path of the protagonist towards full integration into a certain societal structure is of great importance. Both protagonists acquire specific modes of representation related to issues of value, the ability to read signs and to express reality, issues relevant both in the material and poetic economies. Though some similarities exist between the two novels in the area of education, there are also many discrepancies that can help further the interpretation of the works. An insistence on realism in all representation is another common denominator.[12] This insistence on realist representation plays out in different ways in the two novels. I will closely examine their divergent patterns through the lenses of money and economic structures. Thus, both thematic and representational concerns justify the comparison of *Soll und Haben* and *Der Nachsommer*.

Furthermore, in accordance with John Vernon, I believe that some time periods are more suitable for this type of economopoetic interpretation. The nineteenth century was an era of liberalism with pervasive economic and monetary change. It was a time of social, political, and economic change as well as technological improvement, scientific development, and capitalist domination. It is the time Georg Simmel characterizes by an increasing abstraction embodied by money: "Die Steigerung der intellektuellen, abstrahierenden Fähigkeiten charakterisiert die Zeit, in der das Geld immer mehr zum reinen Symbol und gegen seinen Eigenwert gleichgültig wird" (Simmel, 176). In other words, the development from an economy based on the circulation of coins whose exchange value corresponded to the value of their material substance to an economy based on the circulation of alloy and paper currency had an influence on thought. And it is this increasing abstraction – which is central to the idea of realist representation – that I will explore in this book.

As Vernon shows, even though money had always been a topic and theme of literature, some aspects changed during the mid-to-late 1800s. First, money came to replace custom as the major social bond. Second, money itself evolved into something new and unexpected with the growth of banks and the explosion of credit that preceded and accompanied the Industrial Revolution (Vernon, 20). Compared to Britain, industrialization came late to Germany. There was hardly any

12 H. Steinecke (1979) asks if *Soll und Haben* is a realistic novel and decides that it is, at least in the opinion of most of Freytag's contemporaries: "Für die große Mehrzahl der Zeitgenossen und der Kritiker des weiteren 19. Jahrhunderts galt das Werk als realistischer Musterroman; in den Begründungen sind formale, stilistische und darstellungstechnische Argumente auf das engste und unlösbar mit weltanschaulich-ethischen und mit politischen Gesichtspunkten verbunden" (116).

progress during the late eighteenth and early nineteenth centuries. But, as Robert Holub points out, "From 1850 to 1900, however, we find rapid industrial growth accompanied by the concomitant urbanization of society" (Holub, 175). In other words, in Germany, realism and industrial development, with the rise of middle-class economic power, coincide.[13]

The introduction and proliferation of the set of symbolic modes of representation, that is the nature of paper money, was accompanied by a semiotic crisis. In his article "Bild und Schrift: Zur Funktion von Medienwechseln in der realistischen Literatur: Stifter, Keller," Helmut Pfotenhauer points to the changing and increasingly volatile financial climate, concluding that it was accompanied by "einer zunehmenden semiotischen Verunsicherung." He explains: "Die Welt ist nicht mehr einfach lesbar. Deshalb müssen das Lesen und Denken, das Verstehen und Mißverstehen thematisiert werden, will man realistisch schreiben. Der Zeichenrelativismus und die Zeichenskepsis der Jahrhundertwende kündigt sich an; der sogenannte Realismus ist davon nicht abzutrennen" (Pfotenhauer, 217).

Insofar as it pertains to Poetic Realism in the German-speaking countries, Theodor Fontane's essay *Unsere lyrische und epische Poesie seit 1848* is important to my line of argument. Fontane adamantly divorces realism from any aesthetic movements that depict the darker aspects of life (such as poverty or social injustice) stating that, "Diese Richtung verhält sich zum echten Realismus wie das rohe Erz zum Metall: die Läuterung fehlt." It is possible to argue that according to this model the true realist author offers refinement of "nature" in the process of literary production. The author is a craftsperson of sorts who extracts the valuable essence of life and shapes it in the form of *Schrift*. Fontane proposes a realist representational model: "Das Leben ist doch immer nur der Marmorsteinbruch, der den Stoff zu unendlichen Bildwerken in sich trägt; sie

13 Eda Sagarra (2001) discusses the development of the German economy, which started accelerating in the 1850s. Germany's rapid industrialization was fueled by both internal and external factors: "Stimulated by Californian gold and an increase in the money supply, the availability of cheaper credit and good harvests engendered confidence, which led in turn to investment in enterprises rather than, as traditionally, government securities" (238).

schlummern darin, aber nur dem Auge des Geweihten sichtbar und nur durch seine Hand zu erwecken".[14] In other words, while the substance of art already exists in the real world, it can only be seen and presented to the world through the creative processes of the artist.

It is the role of the artist to extract the essence, or truth, from the material world without producing anything that did not already exist. The authorial process consists of the organization and presentation (i.e., making concrete through organized details what would otherwise be an abstraction) of that which is already in existence, unearthing meaning, and assembling an understandable and "readable" aesthetic whole from the chaos of life.[15] In realist art, then, we do not encounter a creative, subjective artist but rather an objective and neutral craftsman who expresses an already existing, but hidden, reality to his audience.[16] The author must first see through the disorder of real life

14 In *Realismus und Gründerzeit: Manifeste und Dokumente zur deutschen Literatur 1848–1880*. vol. 2. p. 100.

15 Ulf Eisele (1976) discusses in depth the different phases of realism and their changing modes of theoretical self-understanding using excerpts from *Deutsches Museum* as well as other programmatic and theoretical texts from the 1900s. In his section on *Poetischer Realismus*, Eisele points out the importance of the *process* by which literature is created. In an attempt to explain the concept of *Verklärung*, one has to take into consideration the idea of "re-creating the world" (*wiedergeschaffene Welt*) in the process of literary production: "Der empirisch fundierte Realismus reduziert die Realität also zunächst auf das ihr Wesentliche und versucht dann, in einem zweiten Schritt, das Wesen zur sinnlich-konkreten Erscheinung zu bringen" (63). The idea of identification between reality and fiction is a crucial issue in the understanding of Poetic Realism. In the first step of the process the author brings out the essential: "Der Schriftsteller dient hier als Goldsucher, der nicht produziert, sondern nur freilegt..." (74). In the second step the author brings together the selected essential fragments not by simply "reentering" the inessential into the narrative, but by imitating the *form* of the inessential: "er ahmt am Essentiellen selbst, so wie er es vor sich hat, die *Form* des Inessentiellen nach" (74–5).

16 Referring specifically to the development of an aesthetics of realism in the 1850s, Russell Berman (1986) concludes that there were concurrent shifts in society and culture after the 1848 revolution that supported this development. There was an emergence of an anti-theoretical discourse which favored "experience over concepts and passive observation over enthusiastic activism" (59). Berman continues: "Real things, not imaginary objects, take priority; hence the literature of realism loses much of the subjective reflexivity and

to distinguish meaning from irrelevance, in order to be able to arrange the meaningful and the irrelevant in a "readable" way and create the verisimilitude of the literary representation.

According to Fontane, the real, material world contains the piece of art. Though simple, this model is rather problematic in that it excludes the production aspects of literature. Literature can never be real in the sense that it is the equivalence of the real world: the written word in its role as translator between the material and literary worlds lies somewhere between the two. The creator of *Schrift* necessarily contributes something in the process of capturing the real world and transforming it into text, a contribution not accounted for in Fontane's essay.

We have to look to the literature of the authors of Poetic Realism to see how they deal with these changing realities and their own paradoxical relationships to the written word. It is not the case that the written word is accepted as a neutral medium in a realist representational model - it is actually often viewed with a measure of suspicion.[17] In fact, both the written word and money are "contaminated" by the respective systems within which they operate. We assign meaning and relate to these systems in many different, and often individualized, ways. They are systems of power and sup-

---

philosophical excursiveness of the pre-1848 writing and adopts a primarily descriptive stance" (60). Berman's point is important and relevant to the narrative of Literary Realism. However, beneath the surface of superfluous description, there is a tendency towards abstraction in both *Soll und Haben* and *Der Nachsommer* which relates to economopoetics. More specifically, both Freytag and Stifter question and undermine their own realist representational model by employing economic structures and content.

17 In his discussion of the *Kunstgespräch* in Georg Büchner's *Lenz*, Robert Holub (1991) claims that it exhibits a "tension between the living word from the oral tradition and the dead letter of the text" (48). This tension is of defining importance to the realist literary tradition. The common denominator of these two traditions, i.e., the one that builds on visual arts (nineteenth century) and the one that focuses on the oral dimension (seventeenth and eighteenth centuries), is that "both attempt to bring literature to life by an appeal to the senses" (47). Büchner's *Lenz* demonstrates, claims Holub, that common to both traditions is the "refusal to deal with literature as the dead letters printed on page" (47).

pression, of poetry and commodity. They are anything we want them to be, and sometimes they seem to acquire lives of their own. Because of the representational instability of the two systems, it is particularly interesting and productive to investigate the ways in which realist authors and theoreticians like Freytag and Stifter deal with problems of representation in the material as well as in the poetic economy.[18]

Since I am assuming that existing economic practices and thought influence literary discourse (in which they are employed as structuring devices and metaphoric language), it makes sense to focus on literature from this time of extensive economic change. The transition to an increasingly abstract and symbolic paper economy is the most compelling argument.[19] It is under the umbrella of this transition that I will explore the realist representational issues in *Soll und Haben* and *Der Nachsommer*. As I have indicated, I will base my economopoetic exploration of the two novels on a set of themes that are simultaneously economic and poetic in nature.

While I recognize that both texts are profoundly ideologized, my assumptions concerning economopoetics are not anchored in any particular political ideas or ideological theories. For example, it is not my goal to expose certain economic inequalities addressed in the

18 In his chapter on "The Business of Realism" Robert Holub (1991) points out that the writers of the 1850s realized that they needed to go beyond merely copying reality to poeticizing reality (195). He uses a quote by Otto Ludwig that calls for a "poetic realism": "Art should not be impoverished reality, but enriched reality ... It should not be half of a world, but an entire world." Holub's reading of this quote is that writers "should strive to create a separate and complete reality in their work" (195). Holub also discusses the tension between poiesis and mimesis. On the one hand, a work of art must be true to reality; on the other hand, the construction of a work of art is enlivened by the writer's fantasy and creativity (196).

19 To be sure, paper money was not particularly common in 1850s Germany. In fact, in 1855 only 19% of the money supply, specifically the *Stückgeldmenge*, consisted of paper money (Sprenger, 179). However, the growing economy of the 1850s and 1860s lead to an increasing need for capital. "Der allgemeine wirtschaftliche Aufschwung, eine liberale Wirtschaftsgesinnung, aber auch das fiskalische Interesse mancher Länder führte in den Jahren 1853–1856 zu einer *Gründungswelle von 'Zettelbanken'*, wie die Notenbanken damals allgemein noch genannt wurden. In den vier Jahren kam es zu 16 Zettelbankenneugründungen, davon allein 9 in 1856" (174).

works, nor do I attempt to interpret the authors' views on economics. Instead, I will explore the monetary structures in the texts by means of thematic areas such as accumulation, production, consumption, circulation, exchange, and preservation. These themes are woven through the works, they are places where the material and poetic economies intersect, and they will be the bases of my interpretation. In addition to elucidating the economopoetics of the texts, my interpretative model will use a filter of economic thinking. My intention is not to focus on the themes, but rather to use them to understand the broader representational frameworks of the novels, and, in particular, the ways in which Freytag and Stifter express issues of literary representation through the discourse of money.

Part One
Soll und Haben: The Pursuit of Bourgeois Material and Poetic Wealth

Introduction

> Der Verkehr stockte, die Werthe der Güter und Waaren fielen, Jeder suchte das Seine zu retten und an sich zu ziehen, viele Capitalien wurden gekündigt, große Summen, welche in kaufmännischen Unternehmungen angelegt waren, kamen in Gefahr. Niemand hatte Lust zu neuer Thätigkeit, Hunderte von Bändern wurden zerschnitten, welche die Menschen zu gegenseitigem Nutzen durch lange Zeit verbunden hatten. Jede einzelne Existenz wurde unsicherer, isolirter, ärmer[...]. Das Land war wie ein gelähmter Körper, langsam rollte das Geld, dies Blut des Geschäftslebens, von einem Theile des großen Leibes zu dem andern (Freytag, 1:371).

This quote from *Soll und Haben* captures the essence of money in the novel. Money is the fuel that keeps the machinery of commercial life going. It is the substance that binds people together in meaningful relationships. It is the lifeblood of the material economy. Without it, human existence becomes isolated, insecure, and deprived of meaning. The role of money is like that of text. It connects and "stabilizes" human existence, and it supplies human stories with meaning.

This chapter explores how money and text create value and meaning in Gustav Freytag's novel. I am examining the many intersections of the material and poetic economies in *Soll und Haben*, because it is precisely at these points of convergence that core representational issues emerge at their fullest. Gustav Freytag aestheticizes and ennobles the German *Kaufmannsstand.*[1] He con-

1 Lionel Thomas (1973) explores bourgeois attitudes in *Soll und Haben* by employing a partly biographical approach. Thomas points to Freytag's own experience within the world of commerce and his knowledge of Poles and Jews. Thomas states that Freytag "does recognize that changes are taking place in the

structs an idealized poetic economy ruled by prominent members of the German bourgeoisie when he contrasts Jewish and aristocratic economic mismanagement to the ethically commendable practices of "true" German merchants. The values presented include a strong work ethic, orderliness, industriousness, reliability, dedication, and so forth.[2] The novel overtly promotes the bourgeois mode of economic as well as aesthetic representation by contrasting the fates and pursuits of Anton Wohlfart and Veitel Itzig, and to some extent the Rothsattel family. In its strict dichotomy between Anton and Veitel, the novel displays its overall simplistic (and anti-Semitic) tendencies.

In spite of these blatantly anti-Semitic, anti-Polish, and anti-aristocratic sentiments,[3] *Soll und Haben* should not be dismissed as

---

world around him and he does attempt to come to terms with these changes in his own prejudiced and (for many) wrong-headed way" (63).

2 T.E. Carter (1968) attributes the enormous commercial success of *Soll und Haben* and its legacy as a "Konfirmationsgeschenk" to its idealization of a certain way of life which focused on German bourgeois virtues. "Besides offering adventure it confirmed the social and political assumptions of a generation" (329).

3 A number of studies of *Soll und Haben* have focused on its anti-Semitism, such as articles by Klaus Christian Köhnke (1989) who basically argues that Freytag was not antisemitic in spite of his "antijüdische Ressentiments" in *Soll und Haben* (130), and by Margarita Pazi (1987) who gives a more varied picture of Freytag's anti-Semitism by focusing on his friendships. Peter Hubrich (1974) writes about Freytag's tendency to idealize the "German" bourgeois ways by employing counter models from the Jewish community, Polish society, as well as the German nobility. Hubrich offers many illustrative examples of Freytag's technique to glorify Anton Wohlfart and the society he personifies, with examples ranging from merchant practices, to concepts of *Bildung*, to physical features. These narrative characteristics are not limited to Anton Wohlfart and the Jewish counter model represented by Veitel Itzig, but includes also the less prominent figures in the novel. Hubrich demonstrates that: "auch diese Nebenfiguren als bürgerliche Gegentypen konstruiert sind und ebenso in ein vereinfachendes Schwarz-Weissbild gepresst erscheinen wie der bürgerliche Held und der ihn kontrastierende jüdische Parvenü" (109). Other Freytag scholars, such as Michael Schneider (1980), have defended Freytag in their attempts to rehabilitate the author. Martin Gubser (1998) gives an excellent overview of how different critics have positioned themselves vis-à-vis Freytag's anti-Semitism.

trivial to the tradition of Poetic Realism in Germany.[4] Freytag's work was viewed as one of the quintessential realist works, and it was also immensely popular in its time and during much of the twentieth century. Despite Freytag's occasionally too simplistic dichotomy between the spheres of the real(ist) and false/evil material and poetic economies, the study of his text offers insights into important representational issues that are at the core of Poetic Realism.

Freytag clearly favors the merchant bourgeoisie and its orderly modes of conducting business. Bourgeois business practices, however, are not limited to the sphere of the economy, but also inform the ideas behind Freytag's preferred modes of representation within the realm of poetics. Only the merchant bourgeoisie internalizes the grand order of the world and finds both a poetic and economic expression for this order. Freytag dismisses both the aristocratic and the Jewish economopoetic modes, the former as overly superficial and romantic; the latter as excessively capitalistic and driven by manipulation. In essence, both modes of expression are devoid of substance. These economic tendencies, as Freytag portrays them, are indicative of the aristocratic and Jewish lack of realist perception and representation in the sphere of the poetic economy.

The system of the preferred realist representation, as put forth in *Soll und Haben*, is based on the idea that the modes of exchange are not immediate. All meaningful relationships are based on written exchanges,[5] and almost all of them involve monetary transactions. Freytag validates these monetary transactions throughout the narrative by assigning poetic qualities to them. There is a clear sense of the poetic aura of interconnectedness between individuals within the material economy. Hence, the system of exchange is to some extent a symbolic one even though the content of exchange is always substantive. At the same time as there is a pronounced recognition of the mediated nature of exchange, both in the material and in the poetic

4 Berman (1986) refutes the idea that *Soll und Haben* is insignificant by stating that the novel is "the epitome of bourgeois thought in its transformation from liberalism to imperialism" (79).

5 The dominance of written documents and the search for them is the starting point for Berman's (1986) interpretation of *Soll und Haben* (82–3).

economy, the dangers of the symbolic exchanges and creation of meaning are highlighted by a constant misreading, forgetting, misplacement, etc., of these documents. It is at the places of divergence from the fine point of equilibrium between the symbols of the documents and their substantive "real" value that realist representation defines itself.

As indicated above, Freytag proposes a straightforward representational model in *Soll und Haben*, categorically denying the legitimacy of any system that does not conform to the bourgeois, realist model. Freytag's failure to venture beyond this schematic and simplistic dichotomy is a strategy whereby he refuses to contend with the inherent problem of realist representation, i.e., the inability of text to represent reality transparently. In that, his weaknesses on the aesthetic level reflect simplifications of the social semantics of his characters.[6] Freytag's principle of dichotomy very clearly offers indications as to the nature of the realist representational model that he proposes.[7]

The idea of dichotomization on which my analysis of *Soll und Haben* rests has been used in interpretations by other critics as well.[8]

6 E. McInnes (1979) sees *Soll und Haben*'s inherent weakness in its "evasion of any attempt to relate the values he invokes to the actual processes which already by the middle of the century were coming to dominate the life of society." And further "Freytag asserts the unchanging significance of the qualities of trust, loyalty and responsibility within a limited and simplified social environment in a way which he claims will be relevant to the experience of the reader in the latter half of the 19th century, but he does not explore how they might interact with and modify the depersonalizing tendencies of contemporary life" (105).

7 Larry L. Ping (2006) discusses how the anti-Semitic tendencies in *Soll und Haben*, illustrated by Veitel Itzig and Anton Wohlfart as contrasting models, relates to Freytag's Liberalism. Ping's perspective as a historian is valuable because it sheds some light on Freytag's political views and to some extent explains his anti-Semitism as part of a greater context. Ping states that Freytag saw "the Jewish Question as part of a larger problem; that is, the transformation of a backward, divided Germany into a modern, unified, bourgeois nation" (111).

8 In *The Smell of Books: A Cultural-Historical Study of Olfactory Perception in Literature*, for example, Hans Rindisbacher investigates the implications of the semi-odorless society that is presented in *Soll und Haben* and *Der Nachsommer* from, as he labels it, the bourgeois age of "sensory repression" (41). Rindis-

As I will demonstrate in this chapter, a significant divide exists in the dichotomy between the idealized economopoetics of Anton Wohlfart's bourgeois economy and Veitel Itzig's shady opportunism. In addition, Freytag sets up similar, equally polarized systems in his conceptualization of the aristocratic and Polish economies.[9]

After investigating the educational pursuits of the protagonist, Anton Wohlfart, and his *alter ego*, Veitel Itzig, I will turn to what they learn about business from their mentors as suggestive of the societal systems of which they strive to become a part. These societal systems

---

bacher's argues that the texts suggest two distinct models for "creating or, more accurately, regaining a lost social center" (37). The novels can be read as an attempt to overcome "the centrifugal powers" in contemporary society (36). In fact, he contends that both *Soll und Haben* and *Der Nachsommer* have a mission – to posit a model to be followed by the (bourgeois) community at large: "This propagandistic feature turns both these realistic novels into ideological projects and reveals (literary) realism's true face: it is not a faithful description of what is, but a projection of what should be" (39). Rindisbacher remarks: "In structural and aesthetic terms, the realism of *Soll und Haben* appears as a sociopolitical project of marginalization and centering, of elevating and lowering aspects and qualities according to their ideological desirability." One example of this textual strategy that Rindisbacher analyzes in his work is the drawing of clear boundaries between different body types: "The tall, slim classical body versus the distorted, bent-over bodies of the marginal figures" (39).

9 According to Russell Berman, *Soll und Haben* is organized into a three-part equation in which the correct form of bourgeois accumulation is contrasted with two countermodels: "the unproductive and hence insufficiently capitalist aristocracy and the excessively acquisitive Jews" (85). These three forms of capitalism each have a counterpart in the sphere of reading and representing reality in three modes of textual strategies of representation. Berman's reading of *Soll und Haben* is structurally similar to my own exploration of the economopoetics of the text, but Berman's focuses more on the communicative relationship with the reader. He also contends that *Soll und Haben* is not a *Bildungsroman*, but a political novel, and that Freytag merely uses Anton's character and intrumentalizes it. On one level, I agree with Berman in regards to Anton's character. In fact, I will argue that his character is flattened. My reading of this phenomenon, though, diverges from Berman's in that I see Anton's development towards complete conformity and conventionality as a part of his development to become a neutral mediator of exchange. Anton becomes money. Berman, on the other hand, sees this instrumentalization as Freytag's way to endorse his own ideology.

encompass both economic and poetic components. In addition to the educational aspects I will examine closely the rules of business, both within Freytag's merchant bourgeois economy and within the aristocratic and Jewish economies. Through the investigation of these economic modes, I will decipher their implications for the sign system, for the idea of representation and *Schriftlichkeit*, and for the concepts of consumption, production, credit, bookkeeping, and exchange within the realist poetic economy.

Textualization through Familial and Financial Ties

During Anton Wohlfart's childhood a connection between his father and the merchant Schröter develops. The relationship is based on a seemingly random incident – Anton's father, an insignificant bureaucrat, found a promissory note showing the indebtedness of a big landowner in Posen to Schröter's firm. Through *Calculator* Wohlfart's submission of the document to its rightful owner, Schröter is able to win a lawsuit and thereby regain the money that would otherwise have been lost. With this act of duty on the part of Anton's father, a strong linkage develops between Schröter's firm in the capital city and Anton's family.[10] The Schröters express their gratitude towards the family by unfailingly sending annual Christmas packages to the Wohlfarts. The relationship between the two families greatly influences Anton's future path to becoming a bourgeois merchant. First, it provides Anton with an alternative career option. From the very beginning it is evident that Anton, in addition to being a *Musterknabe* in general, is a multi-talented young man with many occupational opportunities available to him.

10 Again, the search for lost documents is the premise of Berman's (1986) interpretation of *Soll und Haben*. The circumstance around this incident signifies the "competing strategies of textualization in capitalist culture" (83).

Und da der Zeichenlehrer behauptete, Anton müsse Maler werden, und der Ordinarius von Tertia dem Vater rieht, ihn Philologie studiren zu lassen, so wäre der Knabe seiner zahlreichen Anlagen wegen wahrscheinlich in die gewöhnliche Gefahr ausgezeichneter Kinder gekommen, für keine einzige Thätigkeit den rechten Ernst zu finden, wenn nicht ein Zufall seinen Beruf bestimmt hätte (1:7).

Second, the arrival of the annual Christmas package from the Schröters spreads an atmosphere of "poetische[r] Duft" in the Wohlfart household that transpires from Anton's father to Anton.[11] These moments are also connected with the telling of the story of how the Christmas shipments came about in the first place: "Der Vater erzählte dann gern seinem Sohne die Geschichte dieser Sendungen" (1:7). The father saves all the correspondence with Schröter's firm along with his wife's love letters, as if they were sacred documents. In this instance, the successful human contact between Anton's father and Schröter's firm is simultaneously an example of a successful business relationship. The "poetische[r] Duft" and the written communication converge in a realist "textuality" which is defined both by the textual nature of the epistolary communication and the non-textual, olfactory nature of the poetic scent.

The infatuation of Anton's father with Schröter's firm is so great that he becomes somewhat of an expert at commodity characteristics and prices. At some level, he even identifies with Schröter and with the highly desired existence as a merchant:

[...] er fing an, sich für die Geschäfte der großen Handlung zu interessiren, und studirte in den Zeitungen regelmäßig die Marktpreise von Zucker und Kaffe, welche mit merkwürdigen und für Nicht=Eingeweihte ganz unverständlichen Bemerkungen hinter den politischen Nachrichten standen; ja, er spekulirte in seiner Seele mit als Associé seines Freundes, des großen Kaufmanns, er ärgerte sich, wenn der Kaffe in den Zeitungen flaute, und war vergnügt, wenn der Zucker als angenehm notirt war (1:8–9).

11 Rindisbacher uses the sensual appeal of goods to make a connection between textual and business-related exchanges: "Narrative is trade, trade is narrative." Further, he contends that "The trade process of production, transfer, and consumption is comparable to the narrative as an educational process of experience, transfer, and learning" (49).

It is his father's fascination with the world of commodities that sparks Anton's interest in pursuing a career as a merchant. His father's fascination reaches beyond the commodities *per se* to the idea of interconnectedness: "es war die Poesie dieser gemüthlichen Beziehung zu einem ganz fremden Menschenleben, was ihn so glücklich machte" (1:8). As shown both in this and in the initial quote of the chapter, the idea of interconnectedness between people in the chain of commodity exchange is an important theme in the novel because it holds society together in a defining way and it also provides commercial life with a value added – a commercial life which would otherwise have been without meaning, "poetischer Duft," and textual potential. When these connections are severed in a time of economic downturn, the existence of each person becomes "unsicherer, isolierter, ärmer" (1:371). As the narrative voice emphasizes, these connections and bonds constitute the poesy of the system. The fact that Anton's father accepts the notion of value creation in the system of commodity exchange is an indication that Anton, in his capacity as son and "disciple," is also well suited to participate in this system.[12]

In addition, as is evident from the quote above, the father has the desire and capability to decipher the intricacies of the commodity world as they are presented in the newspapers. This willingness and ability to capture the meaning of an underlying, basic system by decoding the complex, intricate, and sometimes confusing signs of the

12 Alyssa Lonner (2005) looks at Freytag's position between the modern world of progress and traditional German society. She identifies elements in his work which are rooted in the tradition of the fairy tale. Both fantasy and poesy are part the *Soll und Haben* narrative: "Freytag weaves into his best-selling novel fairy tale and fantastical elements in a gesture that appears out of place for realist fiction, and indeed counterproductive to his message of middle-class order and reason" (110). Lonner points to a number of facets in *Soll und Haben*, such as the poesy of the *Comptoir*, its *Riesen*, and Anton's Gipskatze which all connote a realm contrary to the "real" world. While these features in Freytag's writing recalls Romanticism, the main point is that their integration into the narrative provides an additional dimension to Freytag's authorship. There is a similarity between Lonner's approach and my own in that they both bring out elements in Freytag's narrative structure that at first sight seem to undermine his Realism, but at a second glance add layers to his narrative and are indications of "hidden" qualities in Freytag's work.

surface is something that is characteristic of the supreme, realist perception proposed by Freytag. Anton's pursuits revolve around the acquisition of this realist vision that is defined by his business experiences with Schröter's firm and the bourgeois economy. As Berman observes "the economic, or liberal capitalist, and aesthetic, or poetic realist, concerns converge in a condemnation of accident and the insistence on a fundamental law and order" (Berman, 80).

The discussion above shows that the attraction to the bourgeois economy, which Anton and his father experience, is multifaceted. The father exhibits a rational mind capable of deciphering the intricate sign system of the merchant's world of commodities, but at the same time there is an emotional appeal as well. It is no surprise that Anton, a young boy at the time, gravitates towards the emotional. As his father jokingly asks him whether he would be interested in becoming a merchant, Anton enthusiastically embraces the idea. He is seduced by the attractive commodities, personal relationships, and an emotional elation akin to the "poetische[r] Duft" mentioned above.

> Und in der Seele des Kleinen schoß augenblicklich ein hübsches Bild zusammen, wie die Strahlen bunter Glasperlen im Kaleidoskop, zusammengesetzt aus großen Zuckerhüten, Rosinen und Mandeln und goldenen Apfelsinen, aus dem freundlichen Lächeln seiner Eltern und all dem geheimnißvollen Entzücken, welches ihm selbst die ankommende Kiste je bereitet; bis er begeistert ausrief: "Ja Vater, ich will!" (Freytag 1:9).

Clearly, the apparent randomness by which Anton's choice of profession is determined does not correspond to the preferences of realist representation. This prevalence of *Zufall* in Anton's entrance into the bourgeois economy can be interpreted in different ways. First, it could be viewed as an innocent beginning of Anton's journey towards mastery of realist vision and representation. This would make sense because Anton's whole childhood is basically disregarded throughout the entire narrative, so, analogously, this episode of *Zufall* during this phase of his life could also be dismissed. On the other hand, this randomness is perhaps only randomness at first sight. It is feasible that the randomness is something happening on the surface of the plot, but that there is a skeleton of meaning beneath the web of *Zufall*, and that this then is "the revision of a superficial accident by the reassertion of a fundamental law".[13] I contend that Freytag is creating a notion of "naturalness" by employing the category of *Zufall* in the plot. The randomness of the incident appears natural, especially since it is contrasted to the affected pursuits of Veitel Itzig, Anton's counterpart. The second possibility is the most credible one, because it corresponds to the innocence and naturalness that Freytag connects with Anton's character. It also works on the plot level because it reinforces the idea that the novel is not a constructed piece of literature, but rather that it grew "organically" out of reality without mediation or human interference, a corollary of realist *Objektivität.*[14]

Over the years Anton emphatically and repeatedly agrees to devote his life to the realm of the bourgeois economy, and eventually his father travels to the capital city to secure a position for Anton as an apprentice in Schröter's firm. Upon his father's return, Anton embarks on a preparatory track by practicing investing and currency exchange. He does so by literally executing the transactions; by simulating the operations of the real world. Theory is of no consideration; only reality and *Praxis* offer the kind of training he needs to prepare for his entrance into Schröter's firm. Through these types of business simulations and activities, Anton prepares himself to enter the realm of the bourgeois economy.

Anton makes an effort to become proficient in English, i.e., to master the linguistic side of commodity exchange. His acquisition of

13 Russell Berman (1986) contends that the occurrences leading up to Anton's choice of profession all seem to be pure coincidences but then argues to the contrary: He states that this apparent accident is no accident but rather the opposite (82).

14 H. Steinecke (1979) explores the realism in *Soll und Haben* as pertaining to the outlook of Freytag's contemporaries. One of the categories of realism is *Objektivität*, a concept that was understood as the opposite of *Willkürlichkeit.* Another is "das Zurückdämmen des subjektiven Erzählers, seiner Meinungen, Kommentare und Reflexionen, der Tendenz" (113). Also Ludwig Stockinger (1981) has explored Freytag's realism in *Soll und Haben.* Stockinger attempts to answer the question whether *Soll und Haben* is a realistic novel by comparing it to the theoretical intentions connected with programmatic realism specifically, not realism in general. He also relates this discussion of programmatic realism in *Soll und Haben* to political problems and considerations of Freytag's time.

English is a way of gaining another model of exchange of meaning between two language systems. His mastery of commercial terminology, form, and tone is a prerequisite for becoming a mediator of exchange himself. In the initial phases of his employment at the firm, Anton mostly copies letters: "Anton saß auf seinem Platze im Comtoir und kopirte Briefe..." (1:57). His skills allow him to perform this task with increasing transparency, so that eventually he masters the kind of *Schrift* that the realist system prefers. Anton becomes a medium that transparently "copies" one *Schrift* into another, without subjectivity interfering.

One telling aspect of Freytag's rendition of Anton Wohlfart's childhood is the absence of detail. He establishes very few connections between Anton's early formative years and his later accomplishments. There is a general sense that a solid groundwork was laid by Anton's parents, especially his father. Freytag very soon excludes the parents completely from the narrative. After only a couple of pages Anton is bereaved of his mother and then his father. From that point on, his childhood is a closed chapter that seems to deserve no further mention throughout the remainder of the novel. Through his father, Anton is predisposed to acquire the realist vision and representational power that come with an honorable existence as a bourgeois merchant. His mother's influence on Anton carries little meaning; it is the paternal side that has affected Anton's constitution and his desire to become a merchant of the material and poetic economies. This makes Anton's subsequent smooth transition into the patriarchal order of Schröter's firm possible. Moreover, it is most significant that Anton's father leaves a lasting impression of enthusiasm for and a connection with the Schröter company, which eventually will become a substitute family for Anton.

As Hans Rindisbacher has pointed out, the images of the goods that the name Schröter conjures up in the child's imagination – "Zuckerhüte, Rosinen und Mandeln" – are concrete. In the educational process Anton has to advance to an "abstract poetics of links, networks, partnerships, and deals." Rindisbacher understands the project of aesthetic education in *Soll und Haben* as a process both of "de-emphasizing the sensual aspects of reality and desensitizing the perceiving subject" (Rindisbacher, 44). He interprets Freytag's use of business metaphors as a way to describe important changes in education, such as the beginning shift of parameters from perception to information. "Narratives, mostly in printed form, become the medium of transferring somebody's original, concrete experience packaged as knowledge in the medium of language from its origin to the place of reception or consumption. In language, some of the proximity, the sensuous detail, is inevitably lost" (48). He concludes that there is an apparent analogy with the medium of trade, whereby the goods, too, lose some of their original sensuous qualities while in transit.

This tendency towards abstraction has broader implications for the realm of the economopoetic. To some extent, Anton Wohlfart does advance from the concrete images of goods to the abstract poetics of links, networks, partnerships, and deals. Rindisbacher's argument can be refuted, however, because abstraction in the merchant bourgeois economy is judged harshly through its association with the manipulative modes of Jewish capitalism. The abstract poetics of links, or interconnectedness, is acceptable only when the surface pattern of complex links is connected with a system of underlying meaning. This underlying meaning is not viewed as constructed but rather quasi-natural. The educational challenges Anton faces are concerned with the maintenance of a sound representational system that does not threaten linkages between surface and substance, such as the copying of business letters that precludes economic action (or creative action for the artistic realm). In fact, the narrative of *Soll und Haben* never accepts the existence of a mere abstraction in which the sign system is divorced from its origin, as we see it demonstrated by the business transactions of the marginal figures of the novel. Anton faces a complex and intricate path before he is transformed into a true representative of bourgeois economopoetic ideals.

Following his life in the province, Anton embarks on a journey to the capital where he will join Schröter's firm. On the way to the capital, he encounters Veitel Itzig, a former classmate, and the literary figure against whom Anton is contrasted. Itzig is also heading for the capital, but with motives different from Anton's. As Veitel puts it: "Die Leute sagen, daß du gehst nach der großen Stadt, um zu lernen das Geschäft[...]. Du wirst lernen, wie man Düten dreht und Syrup verkauft an die alten Weiber; ich gehe auch nach der Stadt, ich will machen mein Glück" (Freytag 1:21). Veitel's use of Yiddich syntax stands in stark contrast to Anton's endeavors to transform himself into a neutral medium of exchange by perfecting his linguistic clarity. Veitel's grammar has a negative impact on the message being expressed. His language is as "distorted" as his body, i.e., yet another indication of his "unnaturalness."

It is also evident that Veitel has little regard for Anton's future as a merchant's apprentice in the capital. His comment reinforces the idea that Anton will be anchored in reality by executing certain tasks. He will be learning the underlying principles of commodity exchange by participating in tasks that seem trivial to an outsider. Veitel Itzig, on the other hand, has only a diffuse, opportunistic idea of achieving financial success. For him, the means are of no consideration; only arrival at the final goal matters. Even in this initial stage of the novel, it is already evident that Veitel Itzig does not possess the necessary insights to comprehend the ideals of the realist material and poetic economy. He is not interested in acquiring knowledge and learning the hard way. Instead, he is looking for quick access to the secrets contained in documents; secrets that will enable him to become a rich and powerful man by allowing him to appropriate other people's possessions. Itzig proclaims: "Wenn ich nach der Stadt gehe zu lernen, so gehe ich zu suchen die Wissenschaft, sie steht auf Papieren geschrieben. Wer die Papiere finden kann, der wird ein mächtiger Mann: ich will suchen die Papiere, bis ich sie finde" (1:22). It is worth noting that the scenario Veitel is describing runs exactly parallel to what happened "naturally" to Anton's father. He found the documents which led to a fruitful relationship with the *Schröter* firm, but he did so through the workings of *Zufall*. The free will of Anton's father was not part of the equation because the development was bound to happen anyway. Veitel, on the other hand, sets out to pursue the documents and the riches that will ensue. In a sense, then, he will make an effort to create "meaning" artificially by using the documents to manipulate, for example, the realm of (mis)represented ownership.

Within realist economopoetics, the papers and the texts in themselves are meaningless unless their links with reality are maintained or re-established, as in the case of Anton's father. However,

Veitel's fixation with manipulation of texts and with legal documents in particular is something that has no meaningful place in the order of either the realist economic or poetic representational systems. Its only function is as a contrasting foil against which the correct treatment of sign systems is cast.

Both Anton and Veitel arrive in the capital at their future employer's door with documents in their hands; Anton with a letter from his father, and Veitel with a letter from a certain Barach Goldmann, whom Veitel's future boss, Ehrenthal, had asked for a recommendation of a prospective employee for his business operations. The two letters evoke different reactions from the recipients. Schröter carefully reads through the letter addressed to him and then warmly welcomes Anton into the firm: "Wie ein freundliches Licht flog es über das Auge des Kaufmanns, er öffnete den Brief schweigend, las ihn langsam durch, reichte dem bewegten Anton die Hand und sagte: Seien Sie mir willkommen" (1:41). Ehrenthal, on the other hand, pays little attention to the contents of his letter. Instead, he warns Itzig that nothing is set in stone, and that he should not take it for granted that Ehrenthal will employ him. In this first encounter between the young men and their future mentors and father figures the genuine warmth of Schröter stands in stark contrast to Ehrenthal's probing attitude. The encounter between Ehrenthal and Veitel is an early attempt by the two players to stake out their territory in relationship to each other and serves to emphasize "naturalness" of the bond between the Schröters and the Wohlfarts. The document that establishes the bond between Ehrenthal and Veitel, on the other hand, is questioned and open to renegotiation. It is meaningless because it is an artificial creation that does not have a foundation of meaningful relationships to support it.

During the first night, both Anton and Veitel have dreams that are indicative of their hopes and aspirations as they will enter a new, grown-up world. Anton's dreams revolve around him sitting on a big *Waarenballen* (a fixture in Schröter's firm), whereas Veitel discovers in his dream "daß er ein Baron geworden war, welcher von Hirsch Ehrenthal um ein Almosen angeredet wurde" (1:57). Anton relates to the realm of the concrete signs of commodity exchange. His own personal place is a position of control; he is the master of the

Waarenballen and indirectly of the realm of commodity exchange. Veitel's dream, on the other hand, displays his opportunistic inclinations and his need to achieve societal status and recognition.

After this first night, the two young men start working. It is Veitel's goal always to protect his own interests while working for Ehrenthal. "Da Veitel beschlossen hatte, unter allen Umständen Geschäfte für eigene Rechnung zu machen, und Herr Ehrenthal das ebenso gut wußte, wie Veitel, so wurde auf diesen zarten Punkt nicht weiter eingegangen" (1:50). As he carries out his chores for Ehrenthal that next morning, Veitel also concludes a private business deal. Anton, on the other hand, plays the role of a pure and neutral mediator: "Anton saß auf seinem Platze im Comtoir und kopirte Briefe" to acquire "Einsicht in Stil und Sprache seines Geschäfts" (1:57). There is already on this first day of work an apparent discrepancy between Veitel's manipulative schemes and Anton's diligent pursuits to familiarize himself with the language of his business – by which begins the process of understanding the surface code of business in order to eventually comprehend its substantial aspects. The act of copying letters is also an indication of Anton's future role as a mediator and, at times, a passive player in the big game of commodity exchange.

The ways in which Anton and Veitel take part in financial transactions point to a pronounced distinction between two systems of representation. Anton is unquestionably connected with neutrality and distance; his mode of representation is clear and true – a mode not contaminated by subjectivity and bias. This is why he begins by copying rather than writing letters. He is trained to give a "picture-perfect" rendition of reality. In Anton's world, language (specifically stylistics) plays a role because this realistic accuracy relies on the perfect command of the means of presentation: the written word. The written word is a means of expressing the underlying truth that is visible to the trained eye of a participant in the bourgeois economic system.

In contrast to Anton's skills, Veitel arbitrarily assigns prices to the products he sells – often hiding a major flaw or falsely reflecting the value of the particular product. The sole purpose of his exchanges is profit. He also often engages in money lending activities: "er lieh sein eigenes Geld aus und hatte das ungewöhnliche Zartgefühl, nie mehr als fünfzig vom Hundert zu nehmen; er lieh aber nur auf kurze Fristen und nahm am Zahlungstermin statt des baaren Geldes mit großer Bereitwilligkeit jede Art von verkäuflichen Dingen zu einer Taxe, welche er als Sachverständiger am besten selbst machte" (1:117). Two aspects are of interest regarding these money-lending activities. First, Veitel's financial products are not paid for with money but *in natura*. This can be interpreted as a reluctance to accept a definite amount of money. Instead, Veitel buys himself the endless possibility of further exchange (and thereby also profit) by acquiring objects as payment. Operating in this manner means that there are no borders between transactions. They all become interconnected because they overlap. The objects of the first transaction are involved in the second and so forth. Due to this practice, the definitions of the transactions are confounded. Second, Veitel demands a fee for the "service" of being paid in product. In essence, he gets paid twice, which further confuses the transaction. The "borderlessness" of the transactions destabilizes the whole issue of pricing, thereby making it difficult to establish relational stability between participants in exchanges. Consequently, it makes a "realist" representation – a fair, inherently worthy – price impossible. Money becomes an object more of manipulation than of transaction and substance.

The kind of representational "cleanness" that is associated with Anton disappears when the mediator takes charge of the transaction and the material of the exchange, as is the case with Veitel. This analogy can be carried over to the sphere of aesthetics – the material of literary exchange, the written word, loses its independence, and thereby its ability to represent reality in a true and fair way. According to the representational model associated with Anton, the credibility of the written word is still intact, i.e., the conviction remains that it can authentically represent the truths of the real world.

The above observations concerning the childhood of the protagonist and his first encounter with the new patriarchal order of Schröter's firm indicate the characteristics of a pattern that is evident throughout *Soll und Haben*. This pattern builds upon the idea of the dichotomy between the preferred bourgeois ideals and "the other," which in the beginning of the novel is represented exclusively by

Veitel Itzig. As the narrative strand progresses, Freytag presents more counter-models to the bourgeois economy; the perspectives become somewhat more differentiated as he eventually introduces the nobility into the picture. Before analyzing the economopoetic model of nobility, it is important to look more closely at the preferential status of the bourgeoisie and the ideas that it supports concerning both the material and the poetic economy.

Poesy and Commodity Exchange

Anton's world, both in its economic materiality and in its representational mode, is characterized by order, substance, and solidity. At his work place, the products can be seen and touched, as can the sacks of coins: "Jetzt wird die Thür heftig aufgerissen, ein starker Mann, mit einem Geldsacke unterm Arm, tritt ein, er setzt den Geldsack triumphirend auf den Marmortisch und ruft mit dem Ausdruck eines Mannes, der eine gute That vollbringt: Hier bin ich, und hier ist Geld!" (1:160). There is a measure of discipline, regularity, and conformity that all have a "natural" place in the realm of Schröter's firm. Schröter himself warns Anton: "Ihr Leben wird Ihnen bei alle dem mit der Zeit einförmig erscheinen... es ist eine strenge Regelmäßigkeit in unserem Hause..." (1:65). Fink, the aristocrat in the company and future friend of Anton, reiterates this idea: "Sie sind jetzt als Rad eingefügt in die Maschine, und es wird von Ihnen erwartet, daß Sie das ganze Jahr regelmäßig abschnurren" (1:67). The comparison with a machine suggests a man-made device, but the way it operates seems natural. Once the machine has been put in motion, everything else falls into place. Anton is just one of the parts that supports a greater system. Each part, or person, though, is replaceable.[15] This comparison highlights both Freytag's efforts to

15 As Russell Berman (1986) points out, all relationships in *Soll und Haben* undergo commodification: "Individuals are referred to less by their names than

create a seemingly natural system and Anton's gravitation towards the role of a neutral medium of exchange.

Then again, even in its calm, at times monotonous security, Anton's life still has a poetic flair:

> Herr Jordan gab sich redlich Mühe, den Lehrling in die Geheimnisse der Waarenkunde einzuweihen, und die Stunde, in welcher Anton zuerst in das Magazin des Hauses trat und hundert verschiedene Stoffe und merkwürdige Bildungen persönlich mit allen Kunstausdrücken kennen lernte, wurde für seinen empfänglichen Sinn die Quelle einer eigenthümlichen Poesie, die wenigstens ebensoviel werth war, als manche andere poetische Empfindung, welche auf dem märchenhaften Reiz beruht, den das Seltsame und Fremde in der Seele des Menschen hervorbringt (1:68).

The poesy of the products evokes intense emotions in Anton, emotions that coincide in strength with or even exceed those that originate from the sphere of traditional literary sources.[16] Part of the poesy is the interconnectedness between different worlds; the gaze at the foreign and unknown, and the exhilarating feeling that there is a web of human relationships that supports the chain of commodity exchange.

> Diese Bastmatten hatte eine Hindufrau geflochten, jene Kiste war von einem fleißigen Chinesen mit roth und schwarzen Hieroglyphen bemalt worden, dort das Rohrgeflecht hatte ein Neger aus Congo im Dienst des virginischen Pflanzers über den Ballen geschnürt; dieser Stamm Farbeholz war an dem Sande herabgerollt, den die Wellen des mexikanischen Meerbusens angeworfen haben... (1:68–9).

Anton's attraction to the foreign and exotic, however, has to be distinguished from a general fascination with such phenomena. It is

---

by their function. The scribe Pix is called the black pen, and the warehouse porters are leather aprons" (91).

16 Thomas Eicher (1995) investigates the *Poesiebegriff* in *Soll und Haben*, concluding that it is quite differentiated and definitely worthy of further exploration. The categories extend from the connection of poesy with mood, to its importance to the concept of work, *Bildung*, and fairy tales. He argues that the different levels of poesy which Freytag employs enhance the poetic qualities of the novel. The question at the forefront for Eicher is how the poetic nuances on the meta-level impact the linguistic expression found in the novel.

mostly the pattern of commercial interconnectedness that appeals to him. This distinction surfaces in a discussion between Anton and Bernhard, the learned son of Ehrenthal. The two young men become acquainted through their English lessons and subsequently start spending time together. Bernhard is attracted by the foreign, whereas Anton claims that anything new is exciting only until it becomes familiar and *alltäglich*. Bernhard's response to Anton's statement exhibits his misinterpretation of the poetic potential of the bourgeois economy: "Wie arm an großen Eindrücken unser civilisirtes Treiben ist[...] das müssen Sie selbst in Ihrem Geschäft manchmal empfinden, es ist so prosaisch, was Sie thun müssen." Anton fiercely disputes this notion, stating that nothing could be more interesting than commerce: "Wir leben mitten unter einem bunten Gewebe von zahllosen Fäden, die sich von einem Menschen zu dem andern, über Land und Meer, aus einem Welttheil in den andern spinnen. Sie hängen sich an jeden Einzelnen und verbinden ihn mit der ganzen Welt." Anton claims, for example, that trade creates ties between the Brazilian girl who picks the coffee beans and the farmer's son who drinks the coffee for breakfast. Bernhard still does not accept Anton's argument: "Sie haben eine lebhafte Einbildungkraft und sind glücklich, weil Sie Ihre Arbeit als nützlich empfinden. Aber was der höchste Stoff für die Poesie ist, ein Leben reich an mächtigen Gefühlen und Thaten, das ist bei uns doch sehr selten zu finden. Da muß man wie der englische Dichter aus den civilisirten Ländern hinaus unter Seeräuber gehen." Anton reiterates his position based on the idea that the network of people that constitutes the chain of commodity exchange is the source of poetic emotion: "Nein... der Kaufmann bei uns erlebt ebensoviel Großes, Empfindungen und Thaten, als irgendein Reiter unter Arabern oder Indern. – Je ausgebreiteter sein Geschäft ist, desto mehr Menschen hat er, deren Glück oder Unglück er mit fühlen muß, und desto öfter ist er selbst in der Lage, sich zu freuen oder Schmerzen zu empfinden" (1:274–5).

Later in the novel, at the onset of the rebellion in Poland, Anton experiences first-hand the impact of a threatening situation on Schröter's firm. A shipment of goods of great value is on its way into the area where the uprising is taking place. Schröter's mood and his ability to deal with the situation are contagious, and Anton feels again a strong sense of both energy and poesy as he completes his business chores. "Ihm war, als trüge er Sprungfedern an Arm und Bein; seine Feder flog bei den gleichgültigen Geschäftsbriefen, die er zu schreiben hatte; trotz dem Gedanken an die Gefahr, welche in seiner Seele fortwährend Fanfare blies, war seine Fassungskraft nie schneller, sein Stil nie klarer gewesen, nie hatte er so hurtig Provision und Spesen ausgerechnet" (1:376).[17] The whole situation also transgresses into the sphere of textual expression, because clarity arrives in Anton's ability to transform content and ideas into text. In fact, Anton is quite taken by this feeling of exhilaration. This experience is a realization of the poetic greatness of the bourgeois economic system. It is also a true justification of the value of commercial content as literature-worthy: "Mit einer wilden Freude sagte sich Anton: Das ist Poesie, die Poesie des Geschäfts, solche springende Thatkraft empfinden nur wir, wenn wir gegen den Strom arbeiten. Wenn die Leute sprechen, daß unsere Zeit leer an Begeisterung sei und unser Beruf am allerleersten, so verstehen sie nicht, was schön und groß ist" (1:377).

In his conversation with Bernhard, Anton also comments on the moral aspect of business: "Wer ein ehrliches Geschäft hat, kann von unserm Leben nicht schlecht denken, er wird immer Gelegenheit haben, Schönes und Großartiges darin zu finden" (1:275). The core issue here is the inherent standards of morality within the bourgeois economy that uphold its poetic potential. The trained merchant has a sense of appreciation for the intricacies of the personal and product based linkages that make up the system of commodity exchange, and in a sense, for text itself, because this system of linkages constitutes a text.

17 Bernd Bräutigam (1985) explores the poetic components in the economic environment of *Soll und Haben* by relating them to Freytag's and Schmidt's contributions to the *Grenzboten*. The underlying idea is that Freytag proposes the existence of poesy in daily life in theoretical terms and, more specifically, in the realm of commerce. Bräutigam draws the conclusion that Freytag's theoretical articles constitute "eine Absage an die Oppositionsästhetik" and instead propose "das verklärungsrealistische Postulat" which Freytag draws on in *Soll und Haben*. Bräutigam goes on to showing how Freytag brings out the poesy in the daily commercial life in his novel.

This parallel between the superficial level of commodity exchange and the underlying structure of meaningful relationships can be extrapolated to the poetic economy. The realist vision is just that: the ability to comprehend the value of the underlying, basic structure of meaning through the "superficial" level of linguistic exchange. Anton has a natural inclination to appreciate this relationship both in the material and the poetic economy. Throughout his apprenticeship at Schröter's firm this inclination increasingly becomes second nature to Anton. He is always inquisitive, trying to form a concrete relationship with the environments and people that participate in the creation of the poesy of products: "Wenn er sich Mühe gab, die Eigenthümlichkeiten der vielen Waaren zu verstehen, so versuchte er auch durch Lectüre deutliche Bilder von der Landschaft zu bekommen, aus welcher sie herkamen, und von den Menschen, die sie gesammelt hatten" (1:70).

The mercantile poesy that Anton insists on is not a factual circumstance but rather a mental disposition and a special vision that seem to be partly genetic, and partly acquired through exposure to a sound bourgeois environment and to proper training in commodity exchange. Freytag repeatedly idealizes the simple world of the merchant, emphasizing that only a very few chosen people have an understanding of the brilliance and grandeur of this mercantile world:

> Anton stand unter der gemeinsamen Oberhoheit der Herren Jordan und Pix und entdeckte bald, daß er die Ehre hatte, kleiner Vasall eines großen Staatskörpers zu sein. Was die unerfahrene Außenwelt höchst oberflächlich unter dem Namen Commis zusammenfaßt, das waren für ihn, den Eingeweihten, sehr verschiedene, zum Theil Ehrfurcht gebietende Aemter und Würden (1:84–5).

Participation in the bourgeois economy of commodity exchange is equivalent to belonging to a group of select individuals which, unbeknownst to the general public, carries a responsibility not only within that miniature economy but in the outer world as well. The significance of the representatives of the bourgeois economy to the rest of society can be attributed to the participants' ability and responsibility to spread bourgeois capitalist values. According to the core rhetorical message of the novel, these values need to reign if a better society is to be created.[18] *Soll und Haben* is "the epitome of bourgeois thought in its transformation from liberalism to imperialism" (Berman, 79). As Berman points out, despite the its critique of the excessive capitalism of Ehrenthal and Itzig, *Soll und Haben* is first and foremost an "apotheosis of commercial exchange: Mercantile capitalism alone produces wealth, builds character, and holds the nation-state together" (100).

The belief in bourgeois capitalism's ability to provide a system within which these goals can be accomplished permeates the entire narrative. As Freytag describes the mercantile activities taking place in Schröter's firm, he focuses on the constant motion of money that is a prerequisite of commodity exchange. And even though Schröter's firm is always connected with solidity and stability, there is a sense that intense activity and a certain level of commotion as pertaining to money are necessary parts of that system. As Freytag describes *Cassirer* Purzel's handling of money, he uses verbs describing the sounds of money in motion: "umgeben von eisernen Geldkasten, schweren Geldschränken und einem großen Tisch mit einer Steinplatte. Auf diesem Tische klangen die Thaler, klirrte das goldene Blech der Ducaten, flatterte geräuschlos das graue Papiergeld vom Morgen bis zum Abend" and the motion of money then continues as the *Ausläufer* "mit Geldsäcken und Papiergeld den Tag über nach allen Richtungen der Stadt trabte" (Freytag, 1:85–6). Money is the substance that binds together the process of commodity exchange within a bourgeois capitalist system and is analogous to the patterns of human participation and interconnectedness in the production chain.

18 E. McInnes (1979) points out that Freytag had a program for national recovery after the 1848 revolution in mind when he wrote *Soll und Haben* – he wanted to "help the German people find themselves again after the disturbances of the past few years and rediscover their sense of collective confidence and purpose" (100). He also argues that the basis of *Soll und Haben*'s popularity lies in its focus on certain values to which the German public was able to relate. Schröter epitomizes these values in his leadership of the firm: "In running such a firm Schröter has to show not just a highly specialized knowledge of commodities and markets but also qualities of judgement, self-reliance and far-sightedness which draw on the deepest resources of his character" (100).

Industrial Production and Labor

The novel's motto suggests that it should "das deutsche Volk da suchen, wo es in seiner Tüchtigkeit zu finden ist, nämlich bei seiner Arbeit" (1:1). *Soll und Haben* is not about production or proletarian living conditions; rather, as Berman aptly puts it: "it is about the accumulation of goods in the form of commodities and the socialization of the hero into the world of commodity exchange" (Berman, 84–5).

The avoidance of such important topics concerning industry in Freytag's time warrants further investigation. In *Der Erfolgsroman: Zur Kritik seiner poetischen Ökonomie bei Gustav Freytag und Eugenie Marlitt*, Michael Kienzle points out that German industrial production doubled in the decade in which the novel was written as compared to the previous decade, something he considers to be "ein in der Wirtschaftsgeschichte einmaliger Vorgang" (Kienzle, 13). With these facts about the extensive industrial expansion of the time in mind, it seems appropriate to interpret Freytag's motto about the *Volk* and the *Arbeit* literally, i.e., within the framework of labor and industrial production. However, it is apparent that Freytag does not consider industrial production to be particularly important to the concept of work.[19] Work in *Soll und Haben* is limited to the sphere of

19 Paul Jackson (1981) devotes a whole book to the study of the concept of bourgeois work in selected novels of German Realism. He finds *Soll und Haben* interesting mostly because of the intertwined relationship of bourgeois class consciousness and its aesthetics displayed in the novel. "In Soll und Haben erweisen sich nämlich die ideologische Affirmation und die angestrebte Poetisierung der bürgerlichen Wirklichkeit nicht nur als sich gegenseitig ergänzende, sondern als nahezu identische Anliegen des Autors" (152). Jackson also interprets Anton Wohlfart's attitude towards work within the structural framework of the *Entwicklungsroman*, demonstrating how he goes through different phases of development as he performs his work within different societal spheres. In his discussion of Freytag's anti-Semitism in *Soll und Haben*, Jackson seems to dismiss it as *Kapitalismuskritik* (171). He also claims that "die positiven Gestalten des Romans nur in flüchtiger Berührung mit Geldgeschäften gezeigt werden" (175). This is a statement that clearly simplifies, and even neglects, the interesting structural meaning of money in the

commodity exchange within the bourgeois economy. As Kienzle shows, the discrepancy between economic developments during the 1850s and the literary depiction of the economy in *Soll und Haben* is not random but is, in effect, part of its mission, and indeed an important explanation for its success among the readers of that time, as it served the purpose of legitimizing the societal role of the German bourgeoisie.[20]

Though factual descriptions of proletarian labor and industrial production are virtually absent from the story, the idea of production is not excluded entirely from its plot. Through the sphere of the nobility, the reader is exposed to the negative impact of industrial expansion. Nevertheless, the integration of an industrial venture into the plot does not serve any other purpose than to illustrate the superiority of the bourgeois capitalist system. Just as Freytag sets up a dichotomy between the flawed Jewish and the preferred bourgeois capitalist systems, he also creates a scenario of failure by presenting the aristocracy as incapable of productively participating in the economy.

Freytag uses the character of Baron Rothsattel, a distinguished aristocrat of limited wealth, to illustrate his point.[21]

---

bourgeois merchant economy which is at the forefront of my own interpretation of *Soll und Haben*.

20 H. Steinecke (1979) comments on Freytag's understanding of work: "Sie ist für ihn der wesentliche Lebensinhalt und das entscheidende Merkmal bürgerlicher Kultur und Entwicklung. Der Arbeit kommt ein hoher Bildungswert zu, sie vermittelt die bürgerlichen Tugenden und Verhaltensweisen: Fleiß und Ordnung, Regelmäßigkeit und Pflichtbewußtsein. Daher erfahren wir zwar sehr viel von den Voraussetzungen und den ideellen Werten dieser Arbeit, jedoch wenig vom Materiellen" (112). Freytag's focus on work ethics and the economic engagement of the bourgeoisie reflects the liberal movement of his day.

21 H. Rindisbacher (2002) compares Karl Marx and Friedrich Engels' *The Communist Manifesto* to *Soll und Haben*, finding that there are "surprising commonalities in the conceptualization of work and its social implications" (188). Both texts deal with the losses that modernization bring about. However, the great difference between these two texts has to do with the ways in which their authors stratify society: Marx and Engels in terms of social class, and Freytag in terms of national affiliation. Rindisbacher illustrates this difference by using the visualization of a pie: "Freytag's social pie is cut vertically into national slices, rather than into horizontal layers-or-classes" (189). Marx's

The Rothsattel family is first introduced when Anton, on his journey to the capital, becomes infatuated with the glory of the Rothsattel's manor house and the beauty of their daughter. Upon setting sight on the manor house lavish with trees, flowers, cattle, and horses, Anton is rendered speechless and begins to fantasize. The narrator immediately comments on Anton's reaction to the grandeur of the Rothsattel manor house: "Der Respect vor Allem, was stattlich, sicher und mit Selbstgefühl in der Welt auftritt, war ihm, dem armen Sohn des Calculators, angeboren..." (1:15). The reader is again reminded of Anton's inclination to the values and ideas of bourgeois society that he subsequently will learn. He is not yet mature or trained enough to evaluate critically the world of the Rothsattels or to see it for what it is – a shallow and hollow façade.

The idyllic life at the manor house is disturbed by Ehrenthal, who conspires to ensnare Rothsattel in deals involving money and paper transactions. Initially, Rothsattel is hesitant, proudly stating: "Ich mache keine Geldgeschäfte" (1:33). After some convincing the scheming Ehrenthal puts in motion the fall of the nobleman. At first, Rothsattel is intrigued by the "simplicity" and the apparent cleanness of these transactions:

> In diesem Behältniß lagen fünfundvierzigtausend Thaler in neuen weißen Pfandbriefen der Landschaft. Der Freiherr betrachtete die Pfandbriefe mit vieler Zärtlichkeit. Er saß in den ersten Tagen stundenlang vor dem geöffneten Kästchen und wurde nicht müde, die Pergamentblätter nach den Nummern zu ordnen, sich über den reinlichen weißen Glanz derselben zu freuen und die Tilgungspläne für das Capital zu entwerfen (1:75–6).

---

social pie, on the other hand, has abolished national borders, and is layered, but not sliced. Rindisbacher's comparison of these two texts highlights the theme of dichotomization in my own study. In Freytag's creation of a safe bourgeoise haven, he illustrates some of the parallell tendencies in the modern economy discussed by Marx and Engels. However, Freytag affiliates these tendencies with "the other," i.e., Jews and nobility, above all: "While the Marxian flux and decay are visible in *Soll und Haben* (often associated with specific class or ethnic or national groups – the Rothsattels and the nobility, Itzig and the Jews, Fink and the USA), Schröter's business resists these tidal waves of change" (194).

As is evident from the quote, Rothsattel engages in the meaningless and unproductive act of organizing the documents by their numbers. Be that as it may, he soon comprehends the severe conceptual flaws behind this new way of economizing. Through some false sense of security, he allows his expenses to increase while his revenues do not: "Er war verständig genug einzusehen, daß in seiner Speculation ein Fehler gewesen war. Wenn man ein Vermögen durch jährliche kleine Ersparnisse erwerben will, muß man seine Ausgaben einschränken; er aber hatte seine Ausgaben bedeutend vermehrt." This realization that he will not have sufficient capital to cover the family's increased expenses does not evoke the proper responses in him. Instead of dealing with the situation the way a true bourgeois merchant would have, he puts his trust in the random luck that a lottery can offer: "Ja es geschah, daß er auf einem Spaziergang durch die Stadt bei einem Lotterieeinnehmer eintrat und ein Lotterielos kaufte, damit ein gütiges Geschick das gut machen möge, was schadhaft war" (1:77). The proper response would have been to trust his own ability to reduce systematically the discrepancies in his finances by making the necessary changes in his factual life. It is important to note that the type of *Zufall* Rothsattel tries to bring about is diametrically opposite from the kind of seemingly natural *Zufall* that initiates Anton's pursuit towards integration into Schröter's firm. Rothsattel desires to change his fate by relying on the randomness of a possible lottery win in the same way that Veitel pushes his financial luck.

This difference can be further clarified by looking at a conversation between Anton and Bernhard. The topic of the conversation is the ability to save oneself from failure. Anton praises the man who has the ability to withstand all hardship and define his own fate: "das Allerschönste, was diesem Leben den höchsten Werth gibt, ist doch, wenn die Kraft des Menschen größer ist als Alles, was auf ihn eindringt. Ich lobe mir einen Mann, der sich Leidenschaften und ein ernstes Schicksal nicht über den Kopf wachsen läßt, der selbst, wenn er unrecht gethan hat, sich immer wieder herauszureißen weiß." Bernhard's response is an indication of his understanding that sometimes this is not possible; that the chain of events can move the process of failure too far to be salvaged: "Wenn es aber zu spät ist, und wenn die Macht der Verhältnisse stärker wird als er?" Anton in turn does not believe a man should have to be overpowered by the external circumstances that affect his life: "Ich glaube nicht gern an die Macht der Verhältnisse" (1:509–10). The opposite of Anton's ideal is personified by Baron Rothsattel, who is not an agent of his own life and business activities, but merely a puppet influenced by different characters that want to take advantage of him. He is not taking charge of his own life; he is not writing his own book.

Unfortunately, Rothsattel is also incapable of that bourgeois realist vision which would render him capable of seeing beneath the surface of signs and reaching a deeper level of comprehension. Instead of rectifying his precarious situation, Rothsattel is caught in a vicious cycle of new debts and obligations that he cannot escape.

After numerous steps into a cobweb of intrigue, most of which are instigated by Ehrenthal, Rothsattel's situation looks bleaker, demonstrated by the exchange of the white, shiny promissory note that at first had so fascinated him, into old, tarnished documents of lesser value: "Der Freiherr holte seine reich ausgelegte Cassette hervor und legte an die Stelle der schönen weißen Pergamente das dicke, gelbliche, durch viele Hände abgegriffene Actenbündel, welches von jetzt ab sein Vermögen vorstellte" (1:256–7). There is a clear notion that these documents have lost aesthetic value by being handled by many – it is also the case that the tarnished documents signify a lesser financial value than the ones Rothsattel used to own (1:243–4; 255–6). In addition, the richly decorated surface of the container that holds the documents stands in stark contrast to the deteriorating paper and imagery of the old documents. The richness of signifiers on the surface of the container has no correspondence with its contents because the documents have lost both financial and aesthetic value. The prevalence of this richly decorated, beautiful surface is indicative of the kind of attraction the aristocratic characters feel towards shallow and meaningless connections in both their social and economic lives.

The process by which Rothsattel diminishes his assets continues with the construction of a sugar factory on his land. His intentions are good; he wants to secure the future of his family by increasing the revenue of his assets: "so geschieht es nicht um unsertwillen, sondern für die Kinder, für die Familie. Ich will das Gut befestigen bei unserem Hause, ich will seine Einkünfte so vermehren, daß der Herr dieses Schlosses in der Lage ist, auch für die Zukunft der Lieben zu sorgen" (1:339). Once he is finally convinced to build the sugar factory, both by Ehrenthal and by his own false assumptions about the profitability of such a venture, the project almost immediately gets out of hand. Rothsattel is consumed by all the duties that come with this new venture.

For instance, he selects a technician with an excellent theoretical background and many innovative ideas to oversee the project. Regrettably, this individual does not have the practical skills necessary to complete the project in a timely manner. In fact, his main flaw is his desire for constant change: "dem Erwählten wurde von zähen Praktikern nachgesagt, daß er nie eine Fabrik in ruhigem Betriebe lassen könne, sondern durch hastige Einführung neuer Erfindungen die tägliche Arbeit zu oft störe. Daher galt er für kostspielig und unsicher" (1:340). Rothsattel's attraction to this type of thinking is indicative of his own flawed perspective. Instead of creating a scenario whereby the factory can function without interference, he hides behind the security of "artificial" changes and improvements, without comprehending that the prerequisite for a functioning production facility is the basic system of its operations. This is the exact opposite perspective from that of the bourgeois economy, in which the man-made, but "natural" machine was created to operate without interruption, where everything and everyone can, to use Fink's language, "das ganze Jahr regelmäßig abschnurren" (1:67). Rothsattel simply does not possess the proper insight to penetrate the surface structure to achieve an understanding of the underpinnings of the economic principles that support a healthy, bourgeois economy.

The problem is not that Rothsattel lacks the motivation to participate in the capitalist system. As a matter of fact, he is driven to extremes: "Der Freiherr trieb mit Feuer die Anlage seiner Fabrik" (1:340). In reality, the crux of the matter is the imbalance in his devotion to the construction of the sugar plant. Complete dedication to a cause *per se* does not necessarily constitute a weakness within the system of the bourgeois economy as Freytag presents it, but the lack of legitimate purpose that Rothsattel exhibits renders the venture meaningless. In addition, the zealous way in which he pursues the construction of the factory prevents him from being positively engaged with his family – he is simply consumed by the project and therefore neglects his duties as husband and father.

The construction project not only disrupts family life at the manor house, but it also interferes with the aesthetic pleasures that used to be present: "Ordnung und Behagen waren auf dem Gut nicht mehr zu finden [...]. Alle Welt wurde durch die neue Anlage belästigt. Die Baronin verlore eine Ecke des Parks [...]. Der Bedarf der Wirthschaft wurde größer, die Einnahmen drohten geringer zu werden" (1:340–1). It is no surprise that Rothsattel's misconceived relationship to this capitalist venture has repercussions on his finances. He automatically depletes value, when the opposite should really be the case.[22] The accumulation of value is one of the reigning principles of capitalism, but Rothsattel's financial impotence prevents him from adhering to this principle. The factory project starts intruding on his core competencies which are based on the agricultural activities of the manor house, and in turn on his fixed assets that diminish in value due to neglect and unnecessary exposure to financial risk through the different mortgage schemes initiated by Ehrenthal.

The nucleus of the problem is foremost loss of control as the factory venture takes on a life of its own. Rothsattel is merely the instigator who sets the process in motion, a process that subsequently escalates out of control. Following the logic of Freytag's dichotomized economopoetic system, it is fair to assume that this sense of uncontrolled activity is not an acceptable practice within the preferred bourgeois economic system because it does not work *regelmäßig*, i.e., according to the rules of rational economics. In addition, Freytag's idealized system does not sanction this type of economic practice in

22 Russell Berman (1986) states that not all of Freytag's aristocrats are impoverished but all live off resources they are incapable of replenishing: "The aristocrat carries the burden of the familial past; caught in the nexus of tradition and obligations, he cannot act as freely as do the bourgeois capitalist individualists. His economic behavior lacks the same dynamic potential, and when he engages in entrepreneurship, the result is likely to be catastrophic, since his inherited code of aristocratic honor has nothing to do with the world of business" (85).

which the entrepreneur, in this case Rothsattel, becomes a mere observer of the capitalist process. The virtues of the bourgeois merchant are his thorough understanding of the fundamentals of the bourgeois capitalist economy, his vision that sees beneath a surface that might appear more attractive than it really is, his deep involvement in every aspect of the commercial process of commodity exchange, and his ability to arrive at a perfect balance between his familial and business obligations and responsibilities. Rothsattel personally, and by extrapolation as a representative of nobility, breaks all of these bourgeois rules.[23]

In conclusion, production is relevant in *Soll und Haben* only in an indirect way as one of the springboards for Freytag's criticism of the insufficiencies of the nobility.

He contrasts this default system to the preferred and idealized behaviors of the bourgeois merchant. By directing attention away from production and all of its expected complements (such as, for example, inequalities between the classes and other proletarian issues), Freytag creates the idea that capitalist industrial production is marginal and potentially harmful to the bourgeois economy. Also, the industrial economy has neither the poetic nor textual potential of the bourgeois economy.

23 Kenneth Beaton (1976) views Rothsattel's failure as a direct result of his desire to accumulate capital for his family and thereby spare them the necessity of being engaged in work to earn a living (32). For Beaton it is really a social issue relating to the privileges of the nobility. E. McInnes (1979) also views Rothsattel's failure as closely bound up with his sense of class identity. The deciding factor for McInnes, however, is Rothsattel's inability to see his life within the "context of the economic life of society as a whole" (102). Rothsattel's basic error is that he neglects his real economic function (managing his estate) because he craves social status.

Consumption, Wealth, and Pleasure

Consumption is the other side of the coin of production. An increasing consumption of goods accompanies industrial production. Nonetheless, in economic terms, consumers have the choice of either consuming their disposable income or saving it (i.e., accumulating wealth). The issue of commodity consumption has many facets in *Soll und Haben*. In the sphere of bourgeois society consumption is often delicately removed from the novel, and sometimes even clearly suppressed and judged as an unacceptable character flaw. The scenes around the Schröter dinner table, for instance, seldom include any extravagance; the descriptions focus on the behaviors and discussion topics of the participants around the table. Consumption is not only insignificant to socializing within the private realm of the bourgeoisie, it is also absent from its professional interactions. Anton's engagement in the process of commodity exchange is a good example of how removed he is from the actual consumption of goods. It is true that consumption is an intricate part of the initial contact between the Wohlfarts and the Schröters. However, when the Wohlfarts eagerly await the annual Christmas package with its sugar and coffee, which are both products of luxury consumption, it is not the act of consumption *per se* that is relevant to the Wohlfarts, but the poesy of the connection with the Schröters.

For Anton, the poesy of commodities relates to the relationships that constitute the chain of commodity exchange within the bourgeois economy. In his own role as a neutral mediator in this process, Anton has acquired a detached relationship to the use value of the products. Clearly, he has the strength and ability to resist the pleasures of consumption. He views himself as a link in the chain of product circulation, and his personal satisfaction and pleasure are connected to this role.

There is also no real yearning on Anton's part to achieve the kind of financial success that would allow him to participate more extensively in commodity consumption. Work for Anton is more than just a means of making money and thereby gaining access to the realm of consumption. Anton's philosophy is clarified during the annual

Schröter excursion when the whole firm is invited to participate in a festive day dedicated fully to enjoyment. At the conclusion of the day, Anton interferes in a potentially contentious situation between Sabine, Schröter's sister, and Fink, who always mocks bourgeois ideals. Anton intervenes by pointing out that Fink, if truth be told, embodies many of the values he is himself criticizing. "Wir alle, die wir hier sitzen und stehen, sind Arbeiter aus einem Geschäft, das nicht uns gehört. Und jeder unter uns verrichtet seine Arbeit in der deutschen Weise, die du soeben verurtheilt hast. Keinem von uns fällt ein zu denken, so und soviel Thaler erhalte ich von der Firma, folglich ist mir die Firma so und soviel werth." This comment is a rejection of work as a way to monetarize human effort. Anton gives some examples: "Wenn Liebold seine Ziffern ins große Buch schreibt, so sieht er sie mit Genuß an und freut sich über den schönen kalligraphischen Zug, und wenn er Posten einträgt, welche der Handlung besonders vortheilhaft waren, so lacht er in der Stille vor Behagen" (1:309).

Anton insists that the reasons for participating in the system of commodity exchange are not commercial in nature. The reward is, instead, being able to fulfill gracefully, poetically, and successfully the different tasks in the process of commodity exchange. Only the person capable of doing so is worthy of full participation in the bourgeois economy, i.e., to pursue gainfully a profit and to begin the process of acquiring wealth, and thereby also the privilege to consume. The idea of entitlement through proving one's worth and one's capacity to conform to the prescribed system is extremely rigid. Both Anton's development and the strictly hierarchical system present in the novel reinforce this idea.

In the economic counter-model represented by shady figures such as Veitel, Ehrenthal, and Hippus (Veitel's teacher in all things legal) this kind of rigidity is nonexistent. In Veitel Itzig's world, the pure mediation that Anton accomplishes is out of the question. To the contrary, Veitel is driven by the value-added principle; he focuses on making a personal profit in each transaction: "Mit jedem Gange, welchen er für Herrn Ehrenthal that, suchte er einen andern zu seinem eigenen Nutzen zu verbinden, und erwarb dadurch schnell eine Kundschaft..." (1:117).

Veitel's way of thinking about accumulating wealth is focused on the process of mediating sales, of making money by engaging in the chain of commodity exchange: "Unterdeß wollte er Agent und Commissionär werden; er wollte Käufe und Verkäufe vermitteln..." (1:324). At this point in the novel when Veitel begins to think about ways to "collect" more assets, Freytag introduces the word *Capital*. His vocabulary includes expressions like *anlegen*, *verdoppeln*, *verzehnfachen*, all connoting processes within the realm of capitalism (1:322).

This attitude not only constitutes – within the ethical world of this novel – an "immoral" business practice, but it also comments on a certain mode of representation. By acting in its own interest, as Veitel does, the medium "contaminates" the process of exchange. In the realm of realism, the idea of transparency between reality and the literary rendition of this reality self-destructs with a medium that cannot be assumed to be neutral. In a sense, Veitel undermines both the economic principles that Freytag advocates and their counterparts in the poetical economy.

The question concerning the function of the tempting products that are, after all, present throughout the entire novel still remains.[24] In spite of the presence of opulence, Schröter's firm is not a "realm of sensuous experience, as one might imagine when considering all the exotic goods in its cellars and warehouse, *Kolonialwaren* in the true sense of the term" (Rindisbacher, 44). On the contrary, the goods serve as objects of sensory temptation and as such must be resisted. According to Rindisbacher, the project of aesthetic education in *Soll und Haben* can therefore be understood as a "process both of deemphasizing the sensual aspects of reality and desensitizing the perceiving subject" (44).

One specific example of this principle can be found in Karl Sturm's lesson in temptation in the storeroom among all the exotic products. Karl is the son of one of the giant manual laborers of Schröter's firm. He has many practical skills and a strong character,

24 Russel Berman (1986) views products as desirable because they are signs of exchange: "Each commodity and each price is good not for its own sake but only for its contribution to the total profit-making enterprise of exchange" (90).

but is disappointing to his father because of his physical size. In spite of his physical shortcomings, he does become a member of Schröter's firm. Karl's initiation into the firm consists of a test in self-control. His father gives directives:

> Sieh, aus allen diesen Fässern kannst du essen, soviel du willst, kein Mensch wird dir's wehren; Herr Schröter erlaubt dir's, Herr Pix erlaubt dir's, ich erlaube dir's. Jetzt merke auf, mein Kleiner. Jetzt sollst du probiren, wie lange du vor diesen Tonnen stehen kannst ohne hineinzugreifen. Je länger du's aushältst, desto besser für dich; wenn du's nicht mehr aushalten kannst, kommst du zu mir und sagst: es ist genug. Das ist gar kein Befehl für dich, es ist nur wegen dir selber und wegen der Ehre (1:93).

Karl has to find the strength to remain in the presence of the array of products without giving in to the temptation of eating from the ample food bins. The ability to do so defines his maturity and reliability. By passing the test, he has also completed his initiation into the business. His father has now confirmed that his son Karl is *ehrlich* and *praktisch*, prerequisites for approval in Schröter's firm. In direct connection with Karl's passing of the storeroom test, Anton meets Karl's father for the first time and is immediately accepted as *ein guter Kerl*, and is allowed a place in their family. It is no coincidence that Freytag establishes a direct connection between Karl and Anton, because Karl's lesson in denial carries over to Anton, who himself never really enters into temptation. In addition to the implications of this incident in terms of denial and restraint, there is a message that products are not at hand to be enjoyed, but rather, as Berman phrases it, they are "objects of accumulation" (Berman, 91).

The question then arises – why are products attractive? Berman's suggestion that commodities are objects of desire because they are signs of exchange, which carry with them the aura of exotic difference and foreign places and thereby arouse an erotic interest in the perpetual other, is part of the answer (90). As I have pointed out earlier, it is not really the attraction to the exotic *per se* that motivates Anton's participation in the bourgeois economy, but rather the interconnectedness within the system of bourgeois commercial exchange. More specifically, the attraction can be derived from the creation of meaning that accompanies the process of exchange.

Through the execution of commercial transactions of exchange, people's lives are connected in ways that are viewed as meaningful by Anton's economopoetic model. These transactions are instrumental in creating the bourgeois text, which is kept in the *Geheimbuch*.

Taste and smell are inferior to the abstraction of exchange. The idea of exchange offers an endless amount of possibilities, but only commodities that are not consumed can participate in the eternal circulation of goods. Again, the kind of detachment that Anton exhibits in the process of exchange is part of the bourgeois model to which he subscribes. Berman states that Freytag founds his novel on commercial activity, which endows the hero with the proper understanding of the world of details. This bourgeois understanding includes three components: "a recognition of basic laws beneath the surface of empirical events, an aesthetic libidinal desire for commodities as a legitimating motor for acquisitiveness, and a tendentially ascetic suppression of this desire in order to restrict sensuous consumption" (88–9). These three components play a role in the contrastive system that Freytag presents, especially in the comparison between Anton and Veitel.[25] My reading of consumption abstinence in *Soll und Haben* focuses on its defining role in the bourgeois sphere. Consumption abstinence goes hand in hand with Anton's tendency toward neutral mediation in the process of economopoetic exchange that is then connected with true representation.

25 More specifically, Russell Berman (1986) outlines the differences in the following manner: "The Jewish figure is derided for having an excessive concern with detail, which, as a corollary to the accusation of material acquisitiveness, contrasts with the aristocratic failing of insufficient interest in the present. Both traits are, for the realist Freytag, false modes of perception, unable to penetrate beneath the accidents of surface impression into the dynamic of fundamental laws" (87).

Representation, Credit, and Credibility

In *Soll und Haben* there is a clear distinction between the concrete, bourgeois economy as represented by Anton Wohlfart, and the evasive, non-committal business transactions carried out in Veitel Itzig's shady economy. Anton is connected with the substance of "real" money, i.e., gold coins that possess an intrinsic value. Veitel, on the other hand, reigns within the sphere of paper money and legal documents that represent value, but lack valuable substance.

Anton's stable life is contrasted with Veitel's constant physical motion. He roams the streets of the city, looking for prospective victims for his business schemes. Every new transaction results in an often unfairly gained profit. Hippus, his second mentor and father figure after Ehrenthal, assists him further in refining his art of manipulation by teaching him "die tieffsten Geheimnisse des Wechselrechts und der Hypothekenordnung" (1:129). Just like Anton, Veitel also learns by copying the letters of his master, but Hippus who, after their completion, destroys the originals so that nothing but the copy, the signifier that is, remains.

> Jeden Abend nahm Veitel einige kostbare Recepte in seine Brieftasche auf, Formulare zu Documenten, welche zu nichts verpflichteten, und wieder solche, welche zu weit mehr verpflichteten, als sie den Anschein hatten. Zuweilen schrieb der Alte selbst ein solches Kunstwerk vor, und ließ es den Schüler abschreiben, worauf er seine eigene Handschrift sorgfältig am Licht verbrannte (1:129).

The destruction of the original text (and thereby also of the connection between copy and original) can be extrapolated to indicate that also the unmediated relation between the written word and its referent has been destroyed. Instead of ascribing to a "realist" sign-system, Veitel creates his own abstract and arbitrary order through manipulating the written word. He not only breaks the uncomplicated connection between text and reality but, in addition, reiterates the idea of the constructed nature of text/literature. Veitel's pattern of behavior is analogous to the principle that paper money represents value through the print on its surface. The assigned value of each denomination is arbitrary because it has nothing to do with the material of the paper *per se*. In the same manner, Veitel and Hippus construct legal documents that are intended to mislead their prospective contractual partners by misrepresenting their true content or value.

Veitel has even developed the skill to make things look like new again in order to impress prospective customers. In fact, he focuses all his attention on the *Schein* and learns the *Wissenschaft* of: "altes Messing durch Katzensilber blendend zu machen und altem Silber den allerhöchsten Glanz zu geben [...]." and he buys old tail coats and has mastered a technique to make them look new again: "mit einem Schein von Neuheit zu überziehen [...] um seine Käufer zu verblenden" (1:117).

Anton's relationship to representation is quite different from Veitel's. Anton is mostly engaged in the act of copying letters and other documents with utmost care in order to refine his business skills. He truthfully transfers word for word as he diligently goes over the books. In his world, whether work related or private, it is a virtue to stand by one's word. At one point, Anton and his aristocratic friend Fink are out boating. Through conversation it becomes evident that Anton cannot swim, and he warns Fink that he will sink like a stone if something were to happen. The boat does turn over and Anton almost drowns due to his inability to compromise his own word: "Anton sank, seinem Versprechen getreu, ohne weitere Bemerkungen in die Tiefe" (1:141). As the narrative progresses, the business transactions in which Anton is involved become multi-layered and more abstract in nature. In addition, he becomes entangled in more complex relationships that threaten to compromise his honor. Anton's involvement with Fink and the aristocratic circles surrounding him is one of the most evident challenges to his "bourgeois merchant honor."

Subsequently Anton is lured by Fink to participate in dances arranged by and for the nobility. Anton is reluctant, but is infatuated enough with the lifestyle of the aristocracy that he is fairly easily convinced. There are widespread negative reactions from the office to Anton's participation in the dances. Pix, for example, sees "in dem gegenwärtigen Anton eine Art Verräther am Comtoir, an der großen Wage und am Solo" and claims Fink "sei kein passender Gesellschafter für einen soliden Kaufmann" (1:217–18). Anton himself acknowledges that he has changed, as have the attitudes of the people around him:

> Er selbst war nicht zufrieden mit sich und suchte selbstquälerisch Anklagen gegen sich zusammen. Er war ein Anderer geworden. Er war nicht gerade nachlässig in den Arbeitsstunden, aber seine Thätigkeit machte ihm wenig Freude, sie war ihm oft eine Last. Es war ihm begegnet, daß er in seinen Briefen Wichtiges vergessen hatte, ja er hatte sich ein paar Mal sogar in den Preisen verschrieben, und Jordan hatte ihm mit einer kurzen Bemerkung die Briefe zurückgegeben (1:218).

This passage is interesting for two reasons. First, it shows how Anton's changed state of mind takes a toll on his capacity to perform his copying and writing duties. He can no longer be the neutral mediator of exchange that he was trained to be, because he fails to include all pertinent information in his business letters, i.e., both his realist vision and his representational skills are impaired. Second, the mechanism of control by which Anton gives the documents to Jordan for proofreading stands in contrast to Hippus's destruction of the originals. In Veitel's system of representation, there is no system of checks and balances. Therefore, his system is devoid of credibility, both in an economic and a literary sense. Even though Anton is flawed in his capacity as bourgeois businessman at the moment, the system within which he operates is a well-functioning and credible one.

Another feature distinguishing Anton from both Veitel Itzig and Baron Rothsattel is his attitude toward credit. Anton is very prudent with his money and tries to be frugal with what he has. For example, he never asks for cash advances of his salary from Herr Purzel. There is one conversation between Anton and Fink regarding a new outfit for Anton. Fink thinks that Anton needs new clothes for some upcoming social event. Fink tries to convince Anton by suggesting a business approach: "Sieh das Geschäft doch etwas näher an. Was ist diese Tanzstunde? Es ist eine Art Actienverein zur Verbesserung der Waden aller Theilnehmer, du bezahlst deinen Antheil am Stundengeld wie jeder Andere" (1:165).

As Freytag makes clear, Fink's suggestion that investing in one's social worth is a sound strategy is not valid. On the contrary, the author seems to harshly judge relationships that are entered into for the sake of social status only. Though intertwined relationships carry the whole bourgeois system of commodity exchange and make it desirable, purely social ties can result in financial instability. Baron Rothsattel's financial life, for example, starts disintegrating when he and his family start residing in the city in the wintertime. But the major source of his financial problems is "die größere Ausdehnung seiner gesellschaftlichen Verbindungen" (1:239).

In Anton's case, he does not have the money to buy new clothes for the social events, and it is against his principles to borrow money: "Ich möchte aber nichts auf Kredit nehmen..." (1:163). Fink argues that this time Anton has to make an exception to his rule because he needs to increase his social activities. Later, after a period of uncontrolled spending, Anton discovers that he cannot pay off his debt without using the money that his parents left him:

> Er hatte in den letzten Wochen keine Ausgaben eingeschrieben, ängstlich faßte er die Feder und suchte Rechnungen und Erinnerungen zusammen, um das Versäumte nachzuholen. Mit Schrecken entdeckte er, daß seine Schulden zusammen eine Summe ausmachten, welche er nicht tilgen konnte, ohne die kleine Hinterlassenschaft seiner Eltern anzugreifen. Er fühlte sich sehr unglücklich (1:219).

Losing control of one's financial situation becomes detrimental to happiness. Staying in control clearly means keeping a record of all financial transactions. The necessity of *Schrift* in Anton's world of financial order stands in stark contrast to the secretive ways of Veitel Itzig. Manipulating and even destroying records is the reigning principle for him. It is possible to draw a parallel to the standards of the realist literary sphere because the system within the bourgeois economy is one of equilibrium, i.e., of balancing credit and debit in the books so that the system adequately portrays the true state of the matter. The books must reflect the actual financial situation. In the same manner as representation takes shape in the material economy, the ideal form of realist representation exists within the poetic economy of the novel. Like the activity of copying letters in which Anton participates – no additions or subtractions are part of this process but merely an accurate and very precise rendering of the expressed intent of the respective letter – the process of bookkeeping ensures that credit and debit even out in the end, and thereby accurately reflect the financial situation.

Eventually, Schröter becomes aware of the rumors surrounding Anton's activities within the aristocratic circles and confronts him. Sabine defends Anton, stating that: "Aber Wohlfart ist unschuldig, Traugott, das weiß ich bestimmt. Eine solche Lüge ist nicht in seinem Wesen." It is her opinion that Anton is not capable of "mis-representing" reality. In the ensuing conversation with Anton, Schröter emphasizes: "für den Ruf eines Kaufmanns aber gibt es keinen schlimmeren Argwohn als den, daß er durch niedrige Mittel sich einen Credit geben will, den zu beanspruchen er kein Recht hat." He goes on to say: "Sie haben hier und da Ausgaben gemacht, welche Ihre Mittel offenbar übersteigen und jedenfalls unpassend für Sie waren." Schröter categorizes the rumors as "Verleumdungen, [...] welche seine Solidität als Geschäftsmann und die Respectabilität seiner Famile angegriffen haben" (1:220–2). The conclusion to be drawn from Schröter's comments is that Anton's behavior is not only an example of financial irresponsibility, but also one that infringes on his reputation as a businessman, because his solidity and credibility can be questioned as a result of his immature and irresponsible actions. It is fair to conclude that much of this compromise to Anton's reputation as a bourgeois merchant is due to his efforts to conceal, or at least not openly declare his true identity. In addition, the fact that Anton intentionally or unintentionally has given an impression of being wealthier than he is by spending beyond his means adds to his "complicity" in these deceptive acts.

Anton finally decides to distance himself from the aristocratic company of the dances after this serious conversation with Schröter in order to salvage his honor as a businessman. In spite of having been quite a popular fixture at the events, he is soon forgotten by his dance partners. This again shows the superficial nature of the nobility and its ways of interacting. It does not seem to bother Anton that he was so easily demoted and forgotten because he now devotes all his energies to Schröter's business: "Er stürzte sich jetzt mit Leidenschaft in die Arbeiten des Geschäfts." Schröter gives Anton an advance to cover his financial shortcomings. Anton has matured through this process and is now considered to be more independent (1:232–3). However, his infatuation with the nobility, and especially with Lenore, does not completely end until much later. During the siege at the Rothsattel manor house in Poland Anton realizes that he does not belong to that world because it is "fremd und abenteuerlich," indeed a *Täuschung*, and is able to acknowledge that the whole appeal has been lost: "der glänzende Schein zerronnen" (2:251). This is when he feels free at last and understands his true calling in life – that of bourgeois merchant, and, more specifically, that of participant in Schröter's firm.

Parallel to Anton's realization is Veitel's: "er selbst war ein Wissender geworden. Er hatte die geheimnisvollen Recepte gefunden, er hielt das Gut des Freiherrn fest in seiner Hand für sich selbst, und sein Schicksal näherte sich der Erfüllung" (2:334). It becomes obvious that Anton is on his way to a new beginning, whereas Veitel is heading for destruction.[26] For Anton, abandoning the attractive but deceptive surface of an aristocratic lifestyle brings him back to his inherent ability to produce accurate text. Veitel's realization, on the other hand, is the acquisition of the tools to manipulate textual representations of reality.

Whereas Anton's relationship to credit is all about balancing the books, Baron Rothsattel encounters a decline in wealth as he ventures into the sphere of credit. When Rothsattel sees an announcement in the newspaper concerning the bankruptcy of the estate in Poland in which he has invested, he reacts first with despair and then with a kind of realization:

> Oft hatte er gedacht, ob es nicht thöricht war, Andern in der Fremde sein Geld zu lassen und daheim fremdes nur zu theuer zu bezahlen; immer hatte er eine Scheu davor gefühlt, auch dies runde Capital in seine Unternehmungen zu werfen, er betrachtete es als das Witthum seiner Gemahlin, als das Erbteil der

26 E. McInnes points out that Veitel Itzig is portrayed as a man gripped by dreams of a social position which are not "grounded in a real productive involvement in corporate existence" (104). McInnes also states that Veitel is driven by the belief that he can confront society and subdue it by the force of his will. According to McInnes, the desire to challenge social order is evident in Veitel's attitude to the law: "His intellectual energies are directed towards finding ways of using it as an instrument of conflict, of exploiting its forms in order to gain an illicit advantage" (103).

Tochter. Jetzt war auch diese Summe gefährdet, die letzte Sicherheit war verschwunden, Alles um ihn wankte (1:469–70).

Even though he does exactly what Ehrenthal and Veitel do, Rothsattel is on the receiving end of their schemes because of his inability to master the knowledge of the system the way both Anton and Veitel do, albeit in different ways. Whereas Anton shows respect and reverence to his business counterparts at all times, Veitel is generally quite contemptuous in his attitude towards others, especially those whom he manipulates.

Furthermore, Veitel acquires his wealth through credit, i.e., by lending money for interest. His whole life is built around this activity. For example, at the point at which he has established himself as a businessman, some of the appearance of his success originates from objects that he has obtained from those who have been unable to pay their interest: "zwei auffallend schöne Lampen […], eine gelegentliche notwendige Übernahme für nicht gezahlte Zinsen eines Solawechsels" (2:69). Another business contact of Veitel Itzig's, Tinkeles, has reservations about Veitel's corrupt modes of representation and his business practices: "Ich habe gehabt meine Mühe, ihn zu verhindern, daß er mir nicht hat genommen meine Kleider. Er nimmt's von den Lebendigen. Ich mag nichts zu thun haben mit einem solchen Menschen" (2:325). Veitel consumes energy and power from the people with whom he gets involved. He takes more than they are willing to give, and he appropriates those things that are close to a person's integrity and life.

Veitel typically acquires more than the original contract specified and in addition, his acquisitions venture into the private sphere. This transgression or intrusion into other peoples' lives is one of the harsh judgments against Veitel as an individual who violates other people. This is another example of the "borderlessness" of his business practices. They lack the kind of cleanness that connects Anton with the narrative's bourgeois economy. The transactions in which Veitel is involved have a tendency to destabilize the representational framework, in this case, because he accepts payment *in natura*. It is likely that the value of the lamps that Veitel receives as payment does not correspond to the nominal value of the interest payments in question.

We can safely assume that this in kind payment is inflated in favor of Veitel Itzig. These inflationary tendencies are also characteristic of the way in which he expands his wealth, i.e., by means of credit. In economic terms, credit creates money beyond the current money supply available for use in the economy. This in turn puts an inflationary pressure on the economy as a whole. In addition, credit is inflated because it is merely a promise without substance. Using "credit money" is not equivalent to using money that one truly owns. This is why the whole concept of credit is "discredited" in the bourgeois economy.

Bookkeeping and the Fair Price

The activity of bookkeeping has a special flair to it in Anton's bourgeois economy.[27] In Schröter's firm, *Buchhalter* Liebold is given the title *geheimer Minister des Hauses*. He sits in his quiet corner "in einsamer Majestät und geheimnisvoller Thätigkeit. Unaufhörlich schrieb er Zahlen in ein ungeheures Buch, und sah nur selten von seinen Ziffern auf..." (1:85). In the opposite corner rules *Cassirer* Purzel in a perpetual commotion of money. On his stone table, coins and paper money are in constant motion. Liebold's bookkeeping practices seem to control and record the process of commodity

27 Jochen Weiss (2005) discusses the impact of the principles of bookkeeping on non-economic life spheres in *Soll und Haben*, claiming that "Buchführung ist nicht nur eine Darstellungsart für die Ökonomie, sondern ein quasireligiöses Prinzip, das den Gestaltungsrahmen des menschlichen Lebens und Lebens-Regelns spannt" (87). Drawing on among others Max Weber, Walter Benjamin, and Jürgen Habermas, Weiss explains how the basic idea of balancing assets and liabilities (*Vermögen* and *Schuld*) and the tenets of bookkeeping, i.e., time savings, precision, discipline, and authority and hierarchy, spill over into the bourgeois merchant's existence, and in the case of Anton Wohlfart specifically, culminates in his entry into the *Geheimbuch* of Schröter's firm. As part of the equation Weiss enters *Schriftlichkeit*, highlighting its prominence in the system of bookkkeping, and in the business world in general, by exemplifying how Anton and Veitel employ text and writing in very different ways.

exchange of which money is an integral part. It is in Liebold's *Schrift* where the secrets of commodity exchange rest.

The text created by *Disponent* Pix's brush is also connected with authority: "Herr Pix ergriff den schwarzen Pinsel, malte neben der großen Waage Hieroglyphen auf Packleinwand und beherrschte die Hausknechte mit gewohnter Entschiedenheit" (1:375). The act of creating text seems to grant an increased measure of authority to the person endowed with that role. The expression of Pix's privileged position in the firm is his urge to utilize all available space for storing products. This urge for completion is described as a natural process: Pix "vermochte leere Räume im Hause und dessen Umgegend ebensowenig zu vertragen, wie die Luft und die Philosophie einen leeren Raum vertragen wollen. Wo ein Winkel, eine kleine Kammer, ein Treppenverschlag, ein Kellerloch aufzuspüren war, da siedelte sich Herr Pix mit Tonnen, Leiterbäumen, Stricken und allen erdenklichen Stoffen an..." (1:88). His striving for completion and his ideal of filling up space are really attempts to create meaning, to ascribe "meaningfulness" to all empty spaces. However, Pix's position of authority is mostly connected to his relationship with the gigantic men that physically handle the products: "Sie gehörten ganz der Handlung an, waren die regelmäßigen Untergebenen des schwarzen Pinsels..." (1:90). The power of the *Schrift* is all-pervading and not disputable.

In the third book of *Soll und Haben* Schröter is often referred to as *Kaufmann* and is portrayed as the epitome of bourgeois virtue in both his private and business lives. One example of how he exhibits his exemplary behavior is an incident in Poland after he and Anton have won back Schröter's property in a vicious fight with the host (*Wirt*) at the inn. In spite of the offense committed towards them, Schröter insists on paying the bill for the accommodations to become free of debt. "Bezahlen Sie für uns und für die Pferde[...] wir dürfen hier nichts schuldig bleiben" (1:423). This urge to stand by an agreement and to pay what is owed is important. This is partly a principle that is connected to the idea of credit avoidance but it also falls within the realm of bookkeeping because of the transaction that precedes the incident. Schröter and Anton purchased a service, and, as a principle of bookkeeping, they have to pay the appropriate sum of money for that service. In other words, there has to be a price for any service rendered, which has to be paid in full in order to achieve equilibrium in the system. This principle is non-negotiable, as is the idea of accurate representation.

The topic of purchasing services at a fair price is discussed further in connection with Bernhard, Ehrenthal's son. When Anton begins to take English lessons he comes in contact with Bernhard, who will give him a presentation on older English authors. Bernhard is the only character who is a learned man in the traditional sense of the word. He is described as a frail individual: "Es waren feine Züge and ein zarter Körper, kastanienbraunes krauses Haar und zwei graue Augen von freundlichem Ausdruck." When Anton asks for the price of the lesson, he is surprised that Bernhard has not yet considered this issue. It becomes obvious that he has no intention of being paid for the presentation. Anton makes a comment that suggests that he draws the conclusion that Bernhard distinguishes himself from his father in his ways of doing business: "Sind Sie nicht im Geschäft Ihres Herrn Vaters?" (1:271) The implication, of course, is that Ehrenthal is quite greedy and always intent on making as much money as possible.

The above episode is one in a long chain of negative judgments of Bernhard and the intellectual world that he represents. Not only by characterizing him as a weakling, but also by failing to assign a value to his service and thereby his knowledge, Freytag questions the worth of this type of knowledge in the age of the merchant economy. A fair price needs to be part of the commodity exchange process, and, in this case, it is unlikely that a monetary transaction will take place to represent the rendering of Bernhard's service.

Bernhard lives in his father's house because he is essentially excluded from work in the public sector: "da einem jungen Mann von meiner Confession die Anstellung im Staate nicht leicht wird." Bernhard's one sole interest lies is his books. He is clearly consumed by this passion: "Dabei warf er einen Blick voll Liebe auf sein Büchergerüst, stand auf und trat in ihre Nähe, als wollte er sie seinem Gast vorstellen." Anton, on the other hand, even though he acknowledges Bernhard's interest and knowledge, says that this is not the kind of knowledge for which he strives: "Anton las einige goldene Titel und sagte mit einer Verbeugung: 'Das ist für mich zu gelehrt.' Es waren Ausgaben orientalischer Werke" (1:271–2).

In spite of his passion for such languages as Hebrew, Arabic, and Persian among others, Bernhard is aware of his limitations when it comes to expressing their beauty in German. After reading a passage aloud to Anton, Bernhard exclaims: "Nicht wahr, das ist schön? Der Gedanke meine ich; denn die Schönheit der Sprache im Deutschen wiederzugeben, bin ich zu schwach" (1:273). Bernhard is not capable of expressing the beauty of these languages in German; it is almost a way of saying that he has limited capacity as a translator or mediator. This weakness is significant because mediation is the most important process in the novel. Impotence in the area of mediation is a judgment against Bernhard as a member of the intellectual world and it marks him as inadequate in the business world.

With this first visit the friendship between Anton and Bernhard begins. Freytag makes a comparison between the two, emphasizing both Bernhard's refinement in literary taste and Anton's clear and structured mind: "Bernhards Sprachkenntnisse waren größer, und sein Gefühl für das Reizende in fremder Poesie bis zum Uebermaß fein, in Antons Seele war Alles geordnet und sicher. Wenn Bernhard für Byron kämpfte, so vertrat Anton die ruhige Klarheit Walter Scotts, und Beide waren glücklich, als ihre Begeisterung sich vor dem größten dramatischen Dichter vereinigte" (1:280).

Eventually Anton introduces Fink to Bernhard, although he has doubts about their compatibility. In a discussion about Fink's experience with Native Americans, Bernhard and Fink have diverging opinions as to tribal affiliations based on some linguistic detail. Bernhard has apparently studied some tribal languages that enable him to draw these conclusions. He explains his knowledge:

> "Ich habe mich nur ein wenig um ihre (Indian tribal) Sprache bekümmert," erwiederte Bernhard, "es ist ein Zufall, daß ich vor Kurzem einige Wörterverzeichnisse verschiedener Stämme durchgesehen habe."
>
> "Und wozu haben Sie sich die unnütze Mühe gemacht? Es wird dort drüben schnell aufgeräumt; bevor Sie eine Sprache erlernen, ist der Stamm ausgerottet, der sie sprach."
>
> Jetzt wurde Bernhard beredt. Er sagte, daß die Kenntnis der Sprachen für die Wissenschaft die beste Hilfe sei, um das Höchste zu verstehen, was der Mensch überhaupt begreifen könne, die Seelen der Völker (1:282).

This passage illustrates how diametrically opposed Bernhard's and Fink's approaches to life and henceforth to the *Stoff* of literature are. Bernhard lives only through his books.[28] Fink, in contrast, has experienced first-hand all of the foreign cultures and adventures about which Bernhard can only fantasize. Fink even mocks Bernhard's literary knowledge, saying that it is basically useless because it can never stay current; Bernhard's claim that the knowledge of language is the highest of all and the one that brings insight into human existence warrants no further comment from Fink. It is apparent that Fink is not interested in obtaining that kind of insight, while Anton acquires knowledge through books about the foreign cultures that are involved in the chain of commodity exchange. The application of Anton's knowledge, then again, differs from Bernhard's. Outside his very personal space, Bernhard finds no application for his knowledge, partly because he has only limited capacity as a mediator. By contrast, Anton's insights pertain to the chain of commodity exchange and therefore are useful. The key here is the *Umsetzung* of knowledge.

It is intriguing that Freytag connects Veitel Itzig also to the category *Gelehrter*. "Das waren die Entschlüsse, zu denen Veitel kam, und als er seinen Plan überlegt hatte, wie ein Gelehrter das Buch, das er schreiben will, da trug er seine Pfandbriefe unter das Kopfkissen, verschloß seine Thüre, lehnte einen schweren Stuhl dagegen und warf sich erschöpft durch die Anstrengung des Tages auf sein hartes Lager [...]." (1:324). The comparison between Veitel and a learned man is

28 Mark Gelber (1984) categorizes Bernhard's intellectual and literary activites as "eine Art Flucht vor der Wirklichkeit" (42). He writes: "Als Gelehrter ist er kaum noch lebensfähig; seine Bemühungen um die Literatur haben dazu beigetragen, dass Bernhard die Prinzipien der Wirklichkeit des Lebens verkennt und ihnen entgegentritt" (42). Gelber sees Anton as a mediator between two systems of literary preference; on the one hand the French, romantic tradition as preferred by the aristocracy; on the other hand Bernhard's consumed relationship with esoteric, Persian manuscripts: "Anton spielt in diesem Zusammenhang die Rolle des sensiblen Gleichgewichts zwischen den extremen und gefährlichen Polen" (42–3). I agree with Gelber that Anton is located between these systems of literary preference. However, I do not find that he is a mediator *between* them. Instead, Anton's character is a mediator *within* the system of bourgeois economopoetics.

again used to conjure up negative connotations. It is clearly not a good approach because it is too calculated. There is a measure of unhealthy dedication involved and almost an insinuation of sickliness and even death. The process is too secretive and exclusive, and not transparent to the outsider.

Physical labor is judged much more favorably than the human effort necessary for intellectual work. When Anton and his young friend Karl from Schröter's firm are about to part Anton expresses some ideas pertaining to Karl's work and how it should be valued. Anton suggests that Karl stay on to work for Fink as the new owner of the manor house. Anton himself will move on: "Mein Werk ist zu Ende, du bist mitten in deiner Arbeit. Du thust ein Unrecht gegen dich und deine Arbeit, wenn du jetzt scheidest." In answer to Karl's protest to consider his low wages, Anton goes on to comment: "Es ziemt sich, davon zu reden, [...]. denn der Mensch thut unrecht, wenn er sein Bestes, seine Kraft, auf eine Arbeit verwendet, die ihm nicht in dem Grade lohnt, wie seine Thätigkeit verdient." Again, this is a plea for the fair exchange of services for money (1:298).

Anton himself goes quite far in his adherence to the exchange principle. At a later point, when Fink has joined Anton and the Rothsattels at the Polish estate, the horses that Fink has purchased to pull his carriage are being used for farming duties. In accordance with his strict bookkeeping principles, Anton sets up a special account for the horses in which he: "alle Wochen ihre Anzahl Pferdetage gutschrieb" (1:194).

As always, there is a distinct contrast between Anton and Veitel. Whereas Anton has perfected his business stylistics and bookkeeping skills, these are exactly Veitel's weaknesses:

> [...] er gebrauchte die deutsche Sprache mit vieler Fertigkeit, aber es war ein östlicher Hauch darin, mehr Kehlkopf als höhere Grammatik; er schrieb wohl auch Geschäftsbriefe und Rechnungen, aber es war keine Glätte, kein Strich dabei, die Buchstaben waren so zu sagen widerhaarig, und die Perioden waren löchrig und geflickt; und was vollends die Geheimnisse der Buchhaltung betraf, so war er darin wie ein unschuldiges Kind. Dieser Mangel drückte ihn sehr (1:118–19).

In spite of his shortcomings, Veitel pays great attention to his appearance and always dresses well. In addition, he knows the "Courszettel der Börse auswendig" (1:118). He pays attention to all of those details that will provide him with an opportunity to take advantage of margins of which other, less informed people are unaware. To be sure, the bases of Anton's economic reality (such as balancing books and mastering the modes of bourgeois commodity exchange) are not within Veitel's realm.

As indicated earlier, in Anton's world there is an insistence on paying a fair price for services and products. When Veitel first encounters Hippus, his future mentor is busy with *Feder* and *Tintenfaß*, and Veitel consequently pegs him as *Schriftgelehrter*. During the course of their first conversation, it becomes clear that Veitel is exclusively interested in the business applications that Hippus can teach him. He only wants to find someone who can familiarize him with "die Geheimnisse eines guten Stils und der Buchführung" and that "gegen möglichst geringes Honorar, ja vielleicht gegen einen schwarzen Frack, den er durchaus nicht los werden konnte" (1:120).

When Hippus mentions his price of fifty *Thaler* for this service, Veitel reacts with great surprise, if not shock. He does not understand the price. He wonders to himself: "wie man für eine so gewöhnliche Sache, als der Geschäftsstil ist, so ungewöhnliches Geld fordern könne" and then considers whether this price could be the cost of the secret that he is pursuing. Perhaps Hippus is the chosen one, a "Besitzer der Rezepte" (1:125). Veitel approaches Hippus again, asking if he can teach him the art of having luck in business, i.e., always to sell and buy at the best price: "Ich habe gehört, daß man kann lernen die Kunst, wodurch man Glück hat in allen Geschäften, womit man kann machen jede Art von Kauf und Verkauf zu dem besten Preise." This, in fact, is what Veitel wants to learn. Ultimately, what Hippus offers to teach him is: "Gesetzkenntniß und die Weisheit, das Geschäft zum eigenen Vortheil zu benutzen" (1:126–7).

The passages above illustrate Veitel's lack of adherence to the bourgeois economic system of fair commodity exchange and book-keeping. It is his goal to avoid paying for his tutoring if at all possible. What finally convinces him to purchase Hippus's services is his conviction that the old man might be the keeper of the eternal secret of business, the secret that Veitel set out to acquire at the very beginning of his journey to the city. The romantic idea that such a secret exists, and the belief that such a secret can be bought for money, goes against the whole notion of the bourgeois economy, above all because the concept of luck is foreign to Freytag's bourgeois, realist ideals. The reliance on anything other than a systematic business approach is not desirable.

The Feminine Domain

The main female characters in *Soll und Haben* play into Freytag's dichotomized economopoetic system. For the most part, the female characters (Sabine Schröter, Lenore Rothsattel, and, to some extent, Rosalie Ehrenthal) are extensions of the values that reign in their respective spheres of the economy. They are clearly different in their personalities and in their perceived degrees of virtue. In addition, they participate in the male domain to different degrees and in various ways. Their involvement in the economy can at best be categorized as passive. The question is: what implications do these issues have on the economopoetics of the novel?

In Schröter's household, the sister of the owner, Sabine, is considered to be "eine kalte Heilige, deren Herz einer leidenschaftlichen Schwäche unzugänglich war" (1:146). Once every year all the members of the firm devote one entire day to festive pleasures: "Das Haus von T.O. Schröter hatte einen Tag im Jahre, an dem es sich unabänderlich dem Vergnügen ergab. Dies geschah zur Erinnerung an die Stunde, in welcher Herr Schröter als Theilhaber in das Geschäft seines Vaters eingetreten war" (1:296). Sabine plays an important role during this day. The whole group goes on an excursion to the countryside. Sabine is the central figure whom everyone tries to please: "auf beiden Seiten und hinter ihr diensteifrige Herren, alle bemüht, sich mit ihr als dem Mittelpunkt in Verbindung zu halten..." (1:299). She is also the organizer who keeps everything running smoothly. There is a parallel here to the idea presented by Anton that the bourgeois economic system is a cobweb of relationships in which the office of Schröter's firm is the central point. Sabine also constitutes that important center in the leisure activities of the firm and in the household in general. Unmistakably, the household is structurally equivalent to the capitalist system.

Sabine has one place that can be viewed as her domain: her *Schatzkammer*: "Hier herrschte Sabine allein." This is her *regnum* and a "heimliches, herzerhebendes Zimmer" (1:103) full of fine tablecloths, napkins, crystal, and china. This room contains all the necessary attributes of a prominent bourgeois household. There is a system in place in her special room where everything is well organized and documented. All the linens are marked with pink cardboard pieces and neatly placed in wooden cupboards: "Heut stand Sabine noch spät vor dem Tisch, der mit weißer Wäsche belastet war; sie suchte die Nummern des feinen Damasts zusammen, zählte und sortirte Tischdecken und Servietten, band große Bündel mit rosa Bändern zusammen und hing die Nummerkarten daran. Zuweilen hielt sie ein Stück näher an das Licht und sah mit Behagen auf die weißen Arabesken, welche die Kunst des Webers hineingewirkt hatte" (1:103–4). Sabine takes great pleasure in organizing her linens. She enjoys the beauty of the fabrics, the superb craftsmanship, and artistic skill with which they were created.

Sabine's treasury can be viewed as an mirror image of bourgeois society. The household domain, like her collection of linens, is clearly interwoven with wealth and status, which are defining concepts of the bourgeoisie. In addition, this private space reaffirms some of the bourgeois values that are prominent throughout the novel, such as the creating and maintaining of order and the sorting, collecting, and keeping of records. The space is itself a safe haven and separated from the public sphere of bourgeois society. Nonetheless, it would be incorrect to conclude that Sabine is disconnected from the "real world" or that she is superficial because of her preoccupation with these household objects. On the contrary, it becomes apparent that she possesses a great deal of sound judgment as well. At times when there are potentially serious problems in the household (such as the duel between Fink and Anton) Sabine's thoughts are not on her fine linens

– "ihr Damast war vergessen" – but focus on the immediate question at hand (1:105).

Throughout the novel, the impression prevails that, while Sabine is a central figure in the Schröter household, she has no involvement in issues concerning the business. Then again, at the very end of the narrative, as Anton is ready to leave the Schröters for good, he is asked to stay by the owner, who explains Sabine's role in the firm: "Sabine ist seit dem Tode meines Vaters mein stiller Associé; ihr Rath und ihre Willensmeinung haben in unserm Geschäft öfter den Ausschlag gegeben, als Sie wohl meinen. Sie ist auch Ihr Chef gewesen, lieber Wohlfart" (2:401). After Sabine makes a long speech to Anton about her involvement in the firm, and specifically in those matters relevant to Anton's role in it, she asks him "as a business man" to do her a favor: "Und deshalb, mein Freund, komme ich auch jetzt als Kaufmann zu Ihnen und noch einmal bitte ich Sie, eine Arbeit für mich abzumachen. Sie sollen mir ein Conto durchsehen" (2:402). This is the first stage of Sabine's proposal to Anton. Her role in Schröter's firm is basically meaningful and important, even regarding its business aspects. In spite of her significant role in the business, her involvement is unknown and almost unexpected in the outside world. She is confined to a limited, private sphere and does not receive any public recognition of her contribution to the business.

The situation is different with the young noblewoman Lenore. Anton is infatuated with Lenore but realizes her limitations: "Sie hatte nicht soviel gelernt als ein anderes Mädchen, das er kannte, und ihr Empfinden war durchaus nicht so gebildet; aber sie war eine gute frische Natur, kräftig in ihrem Gefühl und ehrlich in ihrem Urtheil." In comparison with Sabine, Lenore falls short, especially in her education. Anton makes an effort to teach her bookkeeping skills so that she can make herself useful at the manor house in Poland but her interest proves to be ephemeral at best. She is responsible for the "Führung der Hausrechnung," but it turns out that her numbers are unreliable: "ihre Rechnung erwies sich unsicher..." (2:59–60). As soon as the weather is sunny, Lenore abandons her bookkeeping chores to go hunting.[29]

Anton also devotes his energy to teaching her history and English but without much success: "die Jahreszahlen konnte sie nicht behalten, die Vocabeln waren ihr schrecklich" (2:60). The educational projects that Anton has in mind for Lenore all revolve around mediation. In the case of the study of a foreign language it is the translation between two languages, and in the case of history it is the mediation between eras of time. Finally, bookkeeping is ultimately the activity of capturing financial data and organizing and translating them into an understandable – and readable – coded system. Lenore fails miserably in all these areas of mediation and translation, showing that she is as impotent as are her father, Veitel, and Bernhard. She simply does not have the dedication, steadfast energy or talent it takes to live up to Anton's bourgeois ideal. This, however, does not end his fascination with her or his attempts to change her.

Lenore thinks and sees in the superficial modes of the "ugly artform" of caricature which fails to depict reality realistically.[30] She says the following about Ehrenthal: "Ich mag ihn nicht dulden[...] er sieht aus wie ein kleiner fauchender Hamster." Her father, Baron Rothsattel, counters: "Es ist wahr, alle diese Geschäftsleute haben etwas Karrikirtes, und es ist bei aller Gutmüthigkeit für unser Einen nicht immer möglich, bei ihren Bücklingen das Lachen zu unterdrücken" (1:257). In addition, the first *Geheimbuch*, i.e., Lenore's, Theone's, and Hildegard's *gemeinschaftliches Tagebuch*, is full of Lenore's caricatures. Apparently, drawing this type of artform is her

29 Mark Grunert (1993) presens the thesis that Anton's relationship with Lenore is impossible not only because of the difference in social class, but because she is wild, uncontrollable, and pure nature: "Die Hauptfeinde des Bürgertums sind in Freytags Roman nämlich genau genommen weder die Juden (Itzig, Ehrenthal) noch die Polen und schon gar nicht der Adel, sondern vielmehr die Verlockungen der *Freiheit* (Fink) und die Versuchungen der *Natur* (Lenore) – zwei Bereiche, die als latente und immer unterdrückte Seiten von Antons Persönlichkeit existieren und damit seine bürgerlichen Ambitionen von *innen* her bedrohen" (137).

30 See Berman's (1986) lengthy discussion of the connection between the aristocracy and the caricature as pertaining to the different modes of textualization in *Soll und Haben* (92–6).

specialty: "Da aber ihre Stärke nicht sowohl war, Gefühle aufzuzeichnen, als vielmehr Gesichter und lächerliche Männchen zu malen, so hatte sie einige Karrikaturen hineingesetzt, und Hildegard, welche Gedichte machen konnte, hatte zu jedem Bild einige Zeilen gedichtet. In dieses theure Buch durfte kein fremdes Auge blicken, niemand durfte das Heiligthum sehen und berühren" (1:198).

In spite of Lenore's inability to express feelings in the *Geheimbuch*, she is able to participate in the theater at the manor house in the countryside where she spends the summer with her friends. Their activities include reading "Theaterstücke mit vertheilten Rollen," sharing of the "zartesten und höchsten Gefühle," dressing up "mit Mänteln, Shawls und Tüchern" in front of the parents "als Publicum," and performing "Charaden in dramatischen Scenen" (1:234–5). Evidently, it is all about pretending, about playing roles in a theater piece. These dramatic activities are portrayed as the epitome of superficiality. In addition, Freytag endows Lenore with rather unconventional and, to her parents, disturbingly rebellious tendencies – she often plays men's parts, dances men's parts, and dresses up like a man: "Natürlich tanzte Lenore immer als Herr, sooft es an Herren fehlte" and, to top it off, appears "bei einer dramatischen Scene zum Schrecken der Mutter sogar selbst als Herr auf, mit einer Reitpeitsche und einem kleinen Bart von Wolle, den sie allerliebst zu drehen wußte" (1:236). It is apparent that Lenore is somewhat androgynous, or at least that she acts according to expected male rather than female roles. She also alludes to her wish to be a man in a conversation with the *Amtmann* at the manor house:

> "Jetzt hat er wohl andere Geschäfte, und wenn die Leute wissen, daß der Herr nachsichtig ist, so spielen sie dem Amtmann Trumpf aus, wenn er sie scharf behandelt. – Sie können scharf sein mit den Leuten, es ist jammerschade, daß Sie kein Herr sind."
>
> "Ja, Sie haben Recht, es ist jammerschade," nickte Lenore beistimmend ihrem alten Freund zu (1:326).

Even Anton makes a comment to this effect. Because of Baron Rothsattel's incompetence, he needs a man who can help restore the economy of the manor house to order. Lenore responds to his comment: “Ja, sehen Sie … das ist mein alter Kummer, unser früherer Amtmann hat mir das auch schon gesagt” (2:91).

When Anton prepares to leave the manor house in Poland, Lenore promises to change in order to meet Anton’s expectations: “Ich werde Ihnen nicht Schande machen [...]. ich werde immer verständig sein, ich werde auch gute Wirthschaft treiben [...]. ich werde sparen. Ich will wieder das Buch machen mit drei langen Strichen auf jeder Seite, ich werde Alles aufschreiben” (2:301). In other words, Lenore will economize and institute a rigid habit of controlling herself and the books. She will also document all pertinent financial information, as is expected in the bourgeois economic system in which Anton has trained her.

Fink, Lenore’s future husband, has diametrically opposite expectations of her: “So wie du bist, Lenore, entschlossen, kühn, ein kleiner Teufel von Leidenschaft, gerade so will ich dich haben und nicht anders. Wir sind Waffenbrüder gewesen und wir werden es in diesem Lande bleiben.” Fink does not want Lenore to dedicate her time to “Frauenarbeit” against her own nature. He goes on to say: “wenn du das Wirthschaftsbuch nicht führen willst, so läßt du es bleiben” (2:395–6). Fink’s attitude goes against everything that Anton has tried to teach Lenore to help her adopt the bourgeois ideals, which he so vehemently promotes.

In Jewish society, as Freytag portrays it, women are segregated from men to a greater extent than in bourgeois society. A woman’s participation in business matters, which does take place in the Schröter firm, although it is kept behind the scenes, does not exist in Ehrenthal’s family. At Veitel Itzig’s engagement party to Rosalie Ehrenthal, the men talk business and: “Die Frauen waren vergessen, und an solche Behandlung gewöhnt, hielten sie feierlich die Theetassen in der Hand, strichen die Falten an ihren Gewändern zurecht und bewegten anmuthig Hals und Arm, daß ihre Ketten und Armbänder im Kerzenlicht blitzten” (2:379–80). Rosalie herself is portrayed as superficial in accordance with the rest of the women at the party. Of her engagement jewels it is said that they will not last the test of time: “Die Steine sollen verbleichen und das Gold unscheinbar werden im Laufe der Jahre” because she is fated to live her life “als geschmückte Puppe” (2:382–3).

Also, the capital that Rosalie can expect to inherit from her father is deemed worthless or at least meaningless: "Dein Loos ist, Einem heimzufallen, der dein Capital heiratet und deine Glieder mit vergnügtem Lachen in Kauf nimmt [...]" (2:383). Rosalie has been "commodified," and it is her fate to participate in commodity exchange. All the capital that Ehrenthal schemed so ruthlessly to accumulate will not benefit Rosalie. Instead, incognito it will join the great flow of money that runs through society and keeps it alive:

> Das Geld aber, welches der alte Ehrenthal durch Wucher und Schlauheit mit tausend Sorgen für seine Kinder zusammengebracht hat, das wird wieder rollen aus einer Hand in die andere, es wird dienen den Guten und Bösen, und wird dahinfließen in den mächtigen Strom der Capitalien, dessen Bewegung das Menschenleben erhält und verschönert, das Volk und den Staat groß macht und den Einzelnen stark oder elend, je nach seinem Thun (2:382).

Money has its own ways. Money, in and of itself, only has value as the life-giving blood of economic life and really only serves the participants of the bourgeois economic system because they are the ones who participate in the appropriate chain of commodity exchange.

In conclusion, the female characters in *Soll und Haben* are mostly affected by money issues, i.e., they have little participatory power in the economic system within which they live. If they are "active" participants (like Sabine Schröter) it is only behind the scenes. In Freytag's simplistic system of correct and false representational modes in the material as well as poetic economies, their worlds reinforce the strict demarcations between the bourgeois, Jewish, and aristocratic economies that Freytag has created within the boundaries of this literary work.

By the end of *Soll und Haben* Veitel is completely ensnared in his own manipulations. His artificial system of signs, with its broken relationship between signifier and signified, has proved worthless. As it turns out, he drowns in the same waters that "swallowed" Hippus when he was killed by Veitel (2:385–6). Anton, on the other hand, gives birth to a new era by marrying Sabine, Schröter's sister and (silent!) business partner. Anton is granted the honor to inscribe his name in the "Geheimbuch von T.O. Schröter und Compagnie" and thereby opening his own *Soll und Haben* (2:403). The diverging fates of the two characters, so simplistically contrasted throughout the narrative, deliver a clear message. The productive and commendable way of life – because *Soll und Haben* definitely projects a moral stance – and the real(ist) representational mode in the material and poetic economy undoubtedly stand victorious at the conclusion of the novel.

Schrift is at the core of the representational dichotomy between Anton and Veitel. Both aspire to learn writing; Anton the correct kind of writing; Veitel a manipulative, speculative kind of writing. Veitel's relationship with Hippus (from whom he acquires the art of writing) is situated within the realm of death. As Peter Pfeiffer points out, while Anton's "natural" writing evokes life, Veitel is connected with death: "Veitel reduziert die Welt auf ihren Tauschwert, auf abstrakte, arbiträre Zeichen: er verzeichnet sie durch Worte und unscheinbare (schriftliche) Zusätze, mit denen er die Transparenz der Schrift auf das, für das sie einstehen soll, zerstört. Damit hebt er die arbiträre Zeichenhaftigkeit der Schrift hervor..." (Pfeiffer, 17–18). Pfeiffer sees an analogy between paper money and Veitel. Anton, on the other hand, relates to gold coins and has acquired a writing ability that supposedly does not allow for undue manipulation of reality.

The comparison between Anton and Veitel in regard to death is another example of Freytag's system of dichotomization. The connection of Anton with gold coins and Veitel with paper money is something I have broached earlier. However, the connection of the two characters with life and death is not as convincing. On the thematic level, it is apparent that Freytag sets up an economopoetics that links Anton with life and Veitel with death, although in light of the flattening of Anton as a literary character and his evolving into a neutral mediator of exchange, one would have to question whether he does not become obliterated and, in fact, a victim to conventionality. Anton is subsumed by the hierarchical system of bourgeois society and ultimately loses individuality. Sabine "rescues" him into a new, productive life in which he upholds capitalist principles as he strives to expand the wealth of the business. Consequently, Anton becomes synonymous with the Schröter household. On some level, losing your individuality in this fashion is the equivalent of death. There is a multitude of examples concerning the dichotomy of life and death with Anton and Veitel posited at opposite ends of the spectrum. Among others, there are references to Veitel's "Vorliebe für schwarze Kleider" (2:69) as if to connote death. Further, in an encounter between Veitel and Hippus, Veitel's mentor and teacher in the mastery of text manipulation of legal documents, Hippus expresses a degree of admiration for his disciple but also accusingly points to Veitel's ruthlessness in his money affairs "wer von dir Geld haben will, der ist verloren. Es wäre ihm besser, er spränge ins Wasser [...]." Later in his conversation with Veitel, Hippus confirms his own connection with death: "Ja, ich bin fest [...]. ich bin nicht von Fleisch und Blut, ich bin Hippus, ich bin der Tod" (2:73). Death and destruction are brought about not only by these ways of conducting business, but also by the type of *Schrift* that they endorse, i.e., the perfected art of manipulating the text surface in order to disguise the substance of the true content.

Veitel's mentoring relationship with Hippus is very different from that between Anton and Schröter. Embittered when his protege doublecrosses him, Hippus calls Veitel a *Rabensohn* and chastises himelf for having taken him under his wing: "Ich habe ihn gepflegt, als er krank war, ich habe ihn Kunststücke gelehrt, ich habe ihn zu einem Manne gemacht, und so lohnt er seinem alten Freund." Then, suddenly, Hippus sees a mirror on the wall in Veitel's office and realizes that it is his own: "In meiner Stube hat er gehangen, der Schurke hat mir den Spiegel gestohlen, er hat mein Glück gestohlen, zur Hölle mit ihm!" (2:343–4). The mirror signifies representation. On one level, it does not matter who looks in the mirror – it projects the same image. By stealing the mirror and with it the reflections it used to hold, Veitel has become Hippus. Anton's reflection is now an added layer, replacing Hippus's image. Losing the mirror renders Hippus powerless and deprived of his earlier abilities to (mis)represent reality. Veitel has not only stolen Hippus's mirror, but also his identity and crucial "secrets" of manipulation that are now in the hands of his disciple.

When Veitel returns, Hippus becomes afraid for his life. At that point, Veitel takes him to the river and drowns him. Veitel soon realizes that he is no longer part of life: "Nicht mehr lebt er, wie andere Menschen, sein Dasein ist fortan ein Kampf, ein gräßlicher Kampf gegen einen Leichnam, ein Kampf, den Niemand sieht und der doch allein seinen Geist beschäftigt. Was er thut in seinem Geschäft, in Gesellschaft mit Lebenden, ist nur ein Schein, eine Lüge [...]. Er weiß, daß er ausgeschieden ist aus der Gesellschaft der Menschen" (2:351–2).

Later on, when Veitel is nearing the end of his life, Ehrenthal, his prospective father-in-law and also his mentor, attacks him in an agitated, demented state. When he enters the room at the festivities to celebrate his daughter Rosalie's engagement to Veitel Itzig, Ehrenthal almost immediately lashes out at Veitel:

> "Seid still," sagte er vernehmlich, "dort steht er, der Unsichtbare. Wir gehn heim vom Begräbniß, und er tanzt unter den Weibern. Wen er ansieht, dem schlägt er die Glieder. Dort steht er!" schrie er laut und erhob sich aus seinem Stuhl. "Dort – dort. – Stürzt Eure Wasserbecken um und flieht in die Häuser. – Denn der da steht, er ist verflucht vor dem Herrn. Verflucht!" schrie er und ballte die Hände und wankte wie rasend auf Itzig zu (2:382).

Veitel flees the room after the attack. When his messenger boy comes, Veitel realizes that his crimes have been discovered. He runs to the river, is drawn into it by Hippus's ghost, and, just like his master, is swallowed by it.

In contrast, Anton brings both life and economic growth. Against the advice of Schröter, he accepts an offer from the Rothsattel family to assist them in financial matters when they move to the manor house in Poland. After Baron Rothsattel's extensive financial speculations and failures, their economic situation is disastrous. In a conversation between Anton and Fink (who later joins Anton at the Rothsattel estate) Fink assumes that Anton has taken on this task because of the lack of money:

> "Da du dich hier als Cassenführer eingedrängt hast, konnte ich mir denken, daß die Casse leer sein würde." versetzte Fink trocken.
>
> "Ja," fuhr Anton fort, "meine Hauptcasse ist ein alter Toilettenkasten, und ich versichere dich, es würde mehr hineingehen, als darin ist. Ich fühle jetzt manchmal einen unbesiegbaren Neid gegen Herrn Purzel und seine Kreide im Comtoir. Wenn ich nur einmal das Glück hätte, eine Reihe grauleinener Beutel zu erblicken, an Banknoten und an eine Mappe mit Actien wage ich gar nicht zu denken." (2:161).

The economy of the manor house is deprived of all the financial substance that was so typical of Schröter's firm. Anton misses the stability and security of that world in which Herr Purzel rules with his *Schrift* and representational system. The world of balancing credit and debit is far removed from the economy at the manor house. Fink continues by questioning Anton: "Und wie ist es möglich, daß du eine solche Wirthschaft erträgst?" (2:162) One reason is Anton's sense of honor; he has taken on a task and will complete it. Another is his infatuation with Lenore, Baron Rothsattel's daughter. In reality he is replenishing the economy of the family Rothsattel who is devoid of substance. In a sense, he is filling it with life, i.e., he is not only building a financially viable agricultural unit at the manor house, but he is also implementing a system that imitates that of the bourgeois economy, a system that reigns within the representational sphere of the realist world.

Anton's sojourn at the Polish manor house is a detour from his path towards mastering the "correct" kind of *Schrift*, i.e., to textualize realistically the bourgeois economy. In due course, Anton will become one with his *Schrift* when he signs his name into the new *Geheimbuch* of Schröter's company. Anton's "incorporation" into the secret ledger of the firm is paradoxical. While, on one level, he gives life to the future text of the firm, on another level, he encounters the death of his own individuality when he signs himself over to this so-called *Geheimbuch.*

The *Geheimbuch* and Poetic Realism

After two years with the firm, the question arises whether Anton should become a partner in spite of his short apprenticeship. The procedure whereby this occurs is somewhat surprising. Though Schröter has already decided that Anton has proven himself enough to become a partner, he still includes all his employees in the decision. He allows them to have the final say in the matter. Unless one interprets this act as merely a perfunctory gesture, it undoubtedly contradicts the hierarchical and patriarchal system that Freytag has built around Schröter, the owner, because this decision should not demand the full and active participation of all the employees of the firm. Once the determination has been made, a room is prepared for the initiation procedure. Anton stands on a special carpet "wie eine Braut vor dem Altare" (1:158), during an initiation procedure which is heavily marked by ritual.

The next day, Schröter announces Anton's partnership in the company. This is done in the holiest of rooms, the room behind the back office. Schröter explains his actions: "Ich habe so gehandelt [...]. weil Sie tüchtig sind, und weil der Brief, den Sie mir bei Ihrem Eintritt in das Geschäft überbrachten, Ihnen ein Credit bei mir eröffnet hat. Es wird Ihnen Freude machen, daß Sie von jetzt ab durch Ihre eigene Thätigkeit Ihr Leben zu erhalten vermögen" (1:161). Here, Schröter refers to the text-based relationship with Anton, which was formed through the letter from Anton's father. This letter created a semi-familial relationship that mitigated the loss of Anton's father. The document also introduced an economic relationship, in which Anton has a positive balance in an account with Schröter. In addition, by becoming a partner after only two years as an apprentice, Anton will receive an income substantial enough to provide for himself and his prospective family. This step is an important one in Anton's journey towards the rights to *Geheimbuch*.

The final step of Anton's integration into Schröter's firm is the inscription of his name in *Geheimbuch*. Anton's road towards this integration into bourgeois economy is long and far from straight. Anton spends various periods of time away from the firm; among others with the Rothsattels at their manor house in Poland. Prior to this, Anton also visits Poland with the mission to protect Schröter's financial interests during the political uprising there. After having salvaged as much as possible of Schröter's assets and business relationships, Anton returns to the firm. There is a great sense of homecoming, almost as of a lost son who finally returns to his father's door: "Unterdeß war auch dem Reisenden zu Muthe wie einem Sohn, der nach langer Abwesenheit in das Vaterhaus zurückkehrt." He is greeted by Herr Pix and his brush. While Pix shakes Anton's hand, his brush takes on a life of its own and paints symbols on Anton's fur coat: "Da eilte Herr Pix bis auf die Straße, schüttelte ihm lange die Hand und bemerkte in seiner Freude nicht, daß unterdeß sein schwarzer Pinsel diese Bewegungen benutzte, um auf Antons Pelz allerlei Striche und Punkte zu malen" (1:488–9). This episode is significant because it is an act of appropriation. The brush, which is described throughout the novel as the preferred tool in Schröter's firm, is a symbol both of text and power. In this instance, the marks on Anton's coat reaffirm the existing relationship between him and Schröter's firm. At the same time, they connect Anton with the correct kind of *Schrift*, i.e., the text of bourgeois capitalism and realism alike. Indeed, Pix marks Anton's person as a piece of paper on which values are inscribed and which then becomes a mediating commodity, like money itself.

Anton returns to find that the financial state of the firm has deteriorated. He recognizes that he has the important task of "healing" the business. In addition to evening out the losses, i.e., to find the balance between debit and credit, Anton needs to replace lost business contacts: "Und er erkannte, daß die Thätigkeit vieler Jahre nöthig sei, um die Verluste wieder auszugleichen und an Stelle der abgerissenen Fäden neue anzuknüpfen" (1:490). It will be his task to write the firm's new stories, to weave a web of associates and of words which, in turn, become part of the future textual reality of the *Schröter Handlung.*

Upon his arrival it becomes clear that Anton's relationship to the firm will deepen. Schröter offers him a new beginning: "Wohlfart, ich wünsche Sie noch fester an dies Haus zu fesseln [...]. Ich weiß, daß ich keinen bessern Mann zu meinem Stellvertreter machen kann." Anton takes great pleasure in this honorable offer: "Als Anton in sein Zimmer zurückkehrte, da fühlte er, was der Mensch nur in wenigen Stunden des Lebens ungestraft fühlen darf, daß er glücklich war, ohne Reue, ohne Wunsch" (1:493). There is a sense that Anton has found his place in life in this pivotal moment of complete bourgeois fulfillment.

It comes as no surprise that Anton is accepted as the natural successor to Schröter: "dem Hausherrn war anzusehen, wie lieb ihm das persönliche Verhältniß zu einem Mann wurde, der so innig mit den Interessen seines Geschäftes verwachsen war, und in dessen frischem und geordnetem Sinn er ein Bild seiner eigenen Jugend erblickte" (1:497). Schröter sees his own younger self in Anton, who incorporates all the characteristics that the bourgeois capitalist system deems valuable. From the quotes above it is also evident that Anton, as previously noted, is merely a component of a great machine. He is almost subsumed by the system of bourgeois capitalism. Freytag uses words like *fesseln* and *verwachsen*. The skills and mindset that Anton has developed over time are prerequisites for his position as a successor in the patriarchy of the firm but his personality is almost obliterated. His ultimate function is to produce economopoetic text within the bourgeois capitalist system. In Freytag's dichotomized world, he can only do so by becoming a neutral mediator in the process of textual exchange. As Anton loses individuality and turns into a neutral mediator of exchange, he simultaneously opens up the process of representation to endless possibilities. Thus, he becomes money, which, thanks to its neutrality and position as general equivalent, has an eternal potential of expressing meaning.

Due to Anton's infatuation with Lenore and the nobility in general, he eventually chooses to abandon his dream of succeeding Schröter and becoming heir to his empire. His colleagues and the Schröter family are in an uproar because of his absence. Baumann eventually agrees to write Anton in order to convince him to return to the firm, but warns the aunt of the house: "aber ich fürchte, verehrte Frau, es wird nicht viel nützen, denn gerade wenn es ihm schlecht geht, wird er den Pflug nicht verlassen, an den er die Hand gelegt hat um Anderer willen," to which the aunt replies: "Er ist nicht vom Pfluge, sondern von der Feder [...] und er gehört hierher" (2:106). From this it is evident that Anton has embarked on an *Irrweg*; first, he is a man of text, not of agricultural labor; second, he is not where he belongs, i.e., within the bourgeois capitalist system. There are several references to Anton's relation to text and the act of writing, specifically the life-giving, "correct" kind of realist text.[31] He is often portrayed as a neutral mediator both in business (the chain of commodity exchange) and in linguistic acts of describing reality and creating stories. As the novel progresses his skills become increasingly refined; Anton as a literary character is flattened as he is elevated to a pure mediator of exchange and, in reality, to text.[32]

After Anton's sojourn at the Rothsattel manor house, he returns to a firm that has gone through some significant changes during his absence: "Er fand die Handlung nicht so wieder, wie er sie verlassen. Durch viele Jahre war hier Alles fest gewesen, jetzt war das Geschäft in unruhiger, schwankender Bewegung. Viele von den alten Verbindungen des Hauses waren abgeschnitten, mehr neue waren angeknüpft. Er fand neue Agenten, neue Kunden, mehr neue Artikel und neue Arbeiter" (2:357). The firm is in need of stabilization, something that Anton will provide.

In spite of his argument with Schröter when he left for the Rothsattel manor house, Anton is now accepted as Schröter's successor. This act of appropriation occurs through the business ledger, the *Geheimbuch*, of Schröter's firm. As compared to the first *Geheimbuch*, i.e., that of the young women of the local aristocracy, the *Geheimbuch* of Schröter's firm is presented as a truly sacred

31 See Pfeiffer (1995) for a more extensive discussion of this aspect.

32 Russell Berman (1986) argues in a similar fashion to myself when he states that Anton as a hero is not an actor but an object of exchange. He "slides back and forth between aristocratic and bourgeois spheres" (83). This line of argument substantiates Berman's contention that *Soll und Haben* is in fact a political novel, not a *Bildungsroman*.

document. As Berman points out, "Therein lies the identity of the enterprise, hidden to all outsiders and preceding all experience, since this book of business determines and defines social organization." (Berman, 99) When Anton returns this final time there is an unusual openness between Schröter and Anton: "Dieser (Schröter) erwähnte Manches, was der Geschäftsmann nur selten seinen Freunden mittheilt, alle wichtigeren Geschäfte, den geringen Gewinn und die großen Verluste des letzten Jahres." At this point there is a mention of the *Geheimbuch*. The good spirits hiding in the house are coming out again as an indication of what will come. It does not take long for Anton to be drawn into the conversation as if he were still an active participant in the firm: "Unvermerkt war Anton in das Geschäft zurückversetzt, schnell machte er alle Stimmungen des Jahres noch einmal durch, wieder röthete sich seine Wange, sein erloschenes Auge erhielt Glanz, und unwillkürlich begann er von den Geschäften der Handlung zu sprechen, als gehörte er noch dazu" (Freytag, 2:317). Anton comes to life again.

During an intimate moment, Sabine asks Anton for a favor: "Sie sollen mir ein Conto durchsehen" and she continues: "Kommen Sie doch, sehn Sie mein Soll und Haben an." And when she opens the book Anton for the first time lays eyes on the words inscribed "unter kunstvollen Schnörkeln [...]. Mit Gott. Geheimbuch von T.O. Schröter." Anton is taken aback: "Es ist das Geheimbuch der Handlung! [...] das ist ein Irrtum." He goes on:

> Nicht Ihr Herr Bruder und nicht Sie können das im Ernst wollen. Verhüte Gott, daß sich ein Anderer an dieses Buch wage als die Herren des Geschäfts. So lange eine Handlung steht, sind diese Blätter für keines Menschen Auge, als für die Augen der Herren, und nach ihrem Tode für die nächsten Erben. Wer in dies Buch gesehen hat, der weiß, was nie ein Fremder erfahren darf. Und diesem Buch gegenüber ist auch der treuste Freund ein Fremder. Als Kaufmann und redlicher Mensch darf ich Ihren Wunsch nicht erfüllen (2:402–3).

Anton's reaction to being asked to look at the *Geheimbuch* is fierce. He seems to feel that there is a spell, as if anyone who comes in contact with this sacred text without legitimate rights has evoked bad spirits. As it turns out, the first ledger is full and, the new, empty book indicates a partnership: "Mit Gott. Geheimbuch von T.O. Schröter und

Compagnie." Sabine announces: "Und der neue Compagnon sollen Sie sein, mein Freund." This scene of *Vereinigung* between Anton and the Schröters continues when Schröter states: "Jetzt halten wir dich, du Schwärmender, in den Blättern des Geheimbuchs und in unseren Armen."

Again, there is an affirmation of the continuous appropriation of Anton. Both familial and business ties connect him with the Schröters. In addition, textually, Anton becomes part of the future story of the firm as he begins to write his own text within the covers of the sacred business ledger. At the very end of the novel Anton's "poetische Träume" turn out to be "ehrliche Träume," i.e., they were not just idealistic dreams but "real" reality and textual reality as well. At this point, Anton opens a new account and begins to compose his own story: "Das alte Buch seines Lebens ist zu Ende, und in eurem Geheimbuch, ihr guten Geister des Hauses, wird fortan mit Gott verzeichnet: sein neues Soll und Haben" (2:403–4). Anton has matured into a state where he is one with himself and his *Schrift*.

The question is: How does the *Geheimbuch* relate to the aesthetic aspects of the novel? The relevance of the *Geheimbuch* has to be viewed in the context of the whole dichotomized system that Freytag sets up in his narrative.[33] In contrast to Veitel Itzig's destructive manipulation of text and its connection to an arbitrary sign system, Anton's text presumes neutrality and an ability to represent reality realistically, as if it were reality itself. *Soll und Haben* categorizes text as good or bad. This categorization has both a moral layer and an aesthetic one. In dichotomizing text this way, Freytag fails to acknowledge the limitations of *all* written texts to express reality. His system does not recognize text as a dead and deadly material, whether it is Anton's or Veitel's because, in its attempts to capture reality, text simultaneously annuls reality at the very moment it is put on paper.

33 Russell Berman (1986) also relates the *Geheimbuch* to the greater issue of textualization: "The realist Freytag, who condemns the aristocratic reduction of life to caricature and the Jewish manipulation of life as finance, praises the bourgeois textualization of existence as a business ledger" (100).

Conclusion

In *Soll und Haben* both plot and characters are defined by economic structures and forms. Money and the familial, societal, and financial relationships it creates are highlighted throughout the novel. Freytag creates an explicit connection between the material and poetic economies. His economopoetic model, indisputably, relies heavily on a principle of simplistic dichotomization between the idealized bourgeois merchant economy and two counter models, the Jewish and aristocratic economies. It is within this system of dichotomization that I have interpreted Freytag's economopoetics.

At the beginning of *Soll und Haben* there is already a focus on the poetic character of the bourgeois merchant economy. Anton is attracted by the "poetic scent" of the system because of the connections that it creates among people (an interconnectedness that at the same time is text). Ultimately, money is the agent that binds this system of human interaction together. The "naturalness" of the system is further reinforced by the moment of coincidence (*Zufall*) that defines Anton's entrance into the bourgeois economy. When Anton is received by Schröter, the letter from Anton's father constitutes a textual bond between them. The naturalness associated with Anton stands in stark contrast to Veitel Itzig's calculated pursuit of the documents that contain eternal business secrets. Within the conceptual framework of Freytag's narrative, Veitel creates meaning artificially and tends towards abstraction in his financial pursuits.[34] He conducts business deals that involve objects as payment, a practice which adds a certain "borderlessness" to the transactions. In Veitel's system it is difficult to establish relational stability between participants in exchanges, hence money becomes an object of manipulation. While Veitel is engaged in manipulative business deals, Anton is copying

34 Christine Achinger (2005) draws a similar conclusion relating to the depiction of Jews in *Soll und Haben* as part of a fragmented and abstract existence, as an early indication of modernity. "In der Welt der Juden ist so im Roman bereits eine Moderne präsent, die die programmatisch-realistischen Vorgaben sprengt, auch wenn sie im Roman noch als partikular und kontingent erscheint" (85).

letters and fastidiously working on his skills as a neutral mediator. The connections between the economic context and its equivalent in the aesthetic economy in regard to representation and exchange are crucial components of the economopoetics of *Soll und Haben*.

The poesy of commodity exchange is an important aspect of the novel. The poetic potential of the bourgeois economy becomes a topic of intense discussion betweeen Anton and Bernhard Ehrenthal. The economopoetic relevance of commodity exchange is its illumination of issues that relate to realist representation. Money holds commodity exchange together just as interconnectedness among people links the parts in the production chain. The realist vision is about understanding the relationship between the superficial level of commodity exchange and the underlying structure of meaningful human relationships. In my reading of *Soll und Haben*, I have focused on the ways in which Freytag aestheticizes the bourgeois economy. His positive description of the bourgeois capitalist economy as defined by a web of human interconnectedness is exclusionary in that it does not take into account the perspective of its (sometimes) unwilling participants. The whole issue of capitalist oppression is being excluded from *Soll und Haben*, which, in turn, compromises Freytag's realism.

There are other examples of Freytag's exclusionary tendencies: *Soll und Haben* does not focus on the modern, mid-nineteenth-century economy. Industrial participation is limited to the nobility and really only used to show their inability to productively participate in the economy. The aristocratic countermodel to bourgeois economopoetics is made explicit by exploiting Rothsattel's "industrial" flaws, which include his trust in the random luck of the lottery, his inability to remain an agent of his own life and business activities, and his neglect of familial obligations. The most telling illustration of his business practices is the beautifully decorated container in which he keeps his fading business documents – the richness of signifiers on its surface does not correspond with its contents, i.e., deteriorating papers which have lost both financial and aesthetic value. It is characteristic of Rothsattel that he squanders and depletes value when he should instead increase it.

Consumption is suppressed in *Soll und Haben*. Commodity exchange is more important than the act of consumption. Again, there is a difference between Anton and Veitel. Anton has a detached relationship to the use-value of products. Veitel transacts by means of a value-added principle, i.e., he adds an unreasonable profit margin in the process of exchange. Therefore, he "contaminates" the process of exchange and cannot function as a mediator of exchange. Anton, on the contrary, shows restraint in consumption. He derives pleasure from acting as a link in the chain of product circulation. Through his participation he will eventually begin the process of accumulating wealth and thereby also gain access to the sphere of consumption.

The concepts of credit and credibility are of interest in the representational model that Freytag presents in *Soll und Haben*. Veitel attempts to create his own abstract and arbitrary order through manipulating the written word; this practice has a parallel in the realm of paper money because (by means of credibility) it operates without connection between substance and symbol. When Veitel practices writing business and legal documents, Hippus, his mentor, destroys the originals so that only Veitel's copy remains. One could argue that they intentionally disrupt the chain of signification. In addition, this faulty system is devoid of checks and balances and thereby of both, economic and literary credibility. Again, there is a clear discrepancy between Veitel and Anton, who always stands by his word. When Anton makes obvious mistakes in his copying, he retrieves the letters to correct his errors. Hence, the bourgeois system strives for equilibrium, i.e., the balancing of debit and credit. Veitel, by contrast, gains wealth through lending money for interest, again contaminating the transactions by receiving objects as interest payments and thereby destabilizing the representational framework. The concept of credit is discredited in *Soll und Haben* partly because it is inflationary in nature and therefore promotes the wrong kind of representation in the realm of the poetic economy. Freytag's harsh judgment against Veitel Itzig's contamination of the equivalency relationships in the material economy is indicative of the author's suspicion of literary abstraction. He portrays abstraction and relational instability as a threat to realist representation.

The urge for equilibrium and accurate representation can further be exemplified by the insistence on paying a fair price for products and services rendered. This equilibrium is expressed in bookkeeping, which is an important tool in Schröter's firm. Veitel's great weakness is his inability to learn bookkeeping. In regard to the payment of a fair price, Bernhard Ehrenthal is presented as the undesirable counter-model. Generally, he has a limited capacity as mediator and translator, and specifically, he renders his tutoring services for free.

The female characters of *Soll und Haben* support Freytag's dichotomized economopoetic system. The bourgeois Schröter family structurally replicates the capitalist system. Sabine Schröter is the center of the household just as the office is the center of human linkages in the chain of commodity production and exchange. In spite of her participation in the management of the company, she receives no public recognition, nor pay, for her efforts – she is merely a silent partner. Compared to Sabine, the aristocratic Lenore displays no capacity for economic or other type of translation and mediation. Her mode of expression is the caricature that reduces and distorts reality. The Jewish Rosalie, finally, is portrayed as a completely passive commodity.

At the end of the novel Veitel, who learned a manipulative and speculative kind of writing, fails and defaults because of his own manipulations. Anton, on the other hand, excels at the "correct" kind of writing and gains access to the *Geheimbuch* of the Schröter company. Veitel is connected with death, Anton with life and economic growth. However, through the flattening of Anton as a literary character, there is a concurrent implicit criticism of the bourgeois system because it requires full assimilation from its participants. The connection of Anton with life therefore becomes paradoxical because his loss of individuality equates his death.

Finally, when he returns to the Schröters, Anton is appropriated by Pix's brush. He is almost subsumed by the system of bourgeois capitalism and experiences a loss of individuality. Anton as a literary character is flattened and turns into a neutral mediator of exchange and simultaneously opens up the process of representation to endless possibilities. He becomes money and exhibits an eternal potential for expressing meaning. Textually, Anton becomes one with his *Schrift* and part of the future story of the firm at that moment when he signs the business ledger.

Part Two
Der Nachsommer: The Economy of Aesthetics

Introduction

> Der Vater hatte auch einen Kasten, in welchem Münzen waren, von denen er uns zuweilen einige zeigte. Da befanden sich vorzüglich schöne Thaler, auf welchen geharnischte Männer standen, oder die Angesichter mit unendlich vielen Locken zeigten, dann waren einige aus sehr alten Zeiten mit wunderschönen Köpfen von Jünglingen oder Frauen, und eine mit einem Manne, der Flügel an den Füßen hatte (Stifter, 1:11).[1]

This quote from *Der Nachsommer* reflects the strong ties between money and aesthetics in the novel. In contrast to *Soll und Haben*, money is here not the lifeblood of the material economy, but accumulated and fixed as aesthetic objects that negate the former role as facilitator of commodity exchange. Stifter focuses on the aesthetic aspects of precious coins from a lost time. These beautiful, antique coins are not meant to participate in any commercial exchange but are to be used exclusively for aesthetic enjoyment. The symbols on the coins conjure up images from classical mythology.

Most interestingly, Hermes – god of commerce and messenger to all the other gods – is depicted on the coins with his winged sandals. The convergence in Hermes (and here he is depicted on a coin which is in itself the incorporation of the metallic substance of money and the aesthetic/linguistic symbol of the value of that coin)[2] of the

1 All quotes from Stifter's *Der Nachsommer* are from Kohlhammer's *Adalbert Stifter Werke und Briefe: Historisch-Kritische Gesamtausgabe* (2000).

2 As I pointed out earlier, Jochen Hörisch (1996) discusses the circular definition of the relationship between heads and tails of coins: The two sides of the coin have to be seen as a unified entity with the one side depicting a prominent head of state and the other the number stating the value of the coin (13). The two sides of the coin converge and lend each other cover. It is also possible to argue that the head of the coin is the aesthetic component and the opposite side the

"hermetic" topics of both commercial and linguistic exchange[3] is precisely at the core of the economopoetic message of *Der Nachsommer*.

The exchange that takes place in *Der Nachsommer* involves cultural artifacts that participate in an exchange over time. These artifacts are being restored, replicated, systemized, and textually "captured" in catalogs. This exchange process is only one of the sites in the novel at which the material and poetic economies cross paths. This chapter will explore the topic of exchange as well as other phenomena that have both economic and aesthetic implications, such as collecting, value, and consumption within Stifter's narrative. The usage of these thematic categories as a framework facilitates the understanding of the core representational components of the novel.

In *Soll und Haben*, the whole thematic framework revolves around business and economics. The socialization of the hero, Anton Wohlfart, into bourgeois capitalist society and his acquisition of a realist vision and mode of expression carry the entire story line. The plot of *Der Nachsommer*, on the other hand, is not about business and commerce: Stifter deals only implicitly with issues relating to the economy. Nonetheless, as I will demonstrate in this chapter, economic practices and structures greatly inform representational issues in *Der Nachsommer* and indeed are central to the concept of aesthetics that Stifter communicates here.

The novel's avoidance of the "real" economy (such as the factories of industrial production) and its simultaneous retraction into a closed autarchic economy as the primary site of aesthetic experience are indicative of Stifter's representational model, which rejects production as well as consumption. Especially the idea of consumption is judged harshly by the narrative. Consumption poses a direct threat to both the aesthetic and the material economy because it feeds into an increasingly uncontrolled circulation of signifiers in the modern,

---

economic. These two sides come together as one in the coin. The figure of Hermes incorporates both sides of the coin in his "poetic" capacity as messenger in combination with his "economic" capacity as god of commerce.

3 My usage of the term "hermetic" topics of exchange refers to Hermes's dual tasks: that as god of commerce, i.e., commodity exchange: and that as "carrier" or transmitter of information, i.e., linguistic exchange.

liberal market economy. By using an autarchic demarcation Stifter attempts to protect his *Nachsommer* economy and its protagonists from the destabilizing peril of consumption.

In this chapter, I will first look at Heinrich Drendorf's youth and early educational pursuits. The educational aspects in this text are of interest in a discussion of realist representation because the protagonist strives to acquire certain competencies in reading signs and producing *Schrift* that represents reality. These aspects, in turn, relate to the economopoetic topics mentioned above as they are enabling the protagonist to engage in an exchange with the world. Ultimately, the mimetic activities Heinrich is involved in as he develops and matures are an integral part of the economopoetics in this text. Therefore, I will explore Heinrich's development of aesthetic capabilities that simultaneously relate to economic structures.

The Father's House and Aesthetic Education

The first sentence of *Der Nachsommer* reads: "Mein Vater war ein Kaufmann" (1:9). It establishes that the existence of the family hinges on the father's participation in business activities and situates him at once, almost as the founding principle of the novel.[4] As the reader finds out, the home is organized according to the rules and preferences of the father. Though far from despotic in nature, he nevertheless defines the family and how its members relate to each other and to the different spaces in the house.

The first rule is that each room has an assigned function and that each object has an assigned place. For example, after the father reads a book in the library he immediately restores order by returning the book to its specific place: "Überhaupt durfte bei dem Vater kein

4 Klaus-Detlev Müller (1971) remarks "Der Bericht über die Kindheit steht ganz im Zeichen der absoluten väterlichen Autorität, die selbst für die Mutter gilt. Die Ordnung – zentraler Inhalt dieser Phase – ist durch die Person des Vaters gebürgt" (124).

Zimmer die Spuren des unmittelbaren Gebrauches zeigen, sondern mußte immer aufgeräumt sein, als wäre es ein Prunkzimmer. Es sollte dafür aber aussprechen, zu was es besonders bestimmt sei" (1:11). This idea of orderliness and purity runs through the whole *Nachsommer* narrative and is one of the basic principles whereby both pragmatic and aesthetic aspects of life are organized. Actually, the process of arranging, cataloguing, and creating order in the concrete *Lebenswelt* (i.e., the household, Heinrich's scientific research, and the realm of artifacts) is an integral part of Stifter's aesthetic thought.

The father elaborates further on the importance of having one specifically defined purpose: "Jedes Ding und jeder Mensch, pflegte er zu sagen, könne nur eines sein, dieses aber muß er ganz sein" (1:11). The father strongly pronounces the idea of being a unified self and of devoting oneself to one thing, but just as decisively acts against it as he proclaims that Heinrich shall become a "Wissenschafter im Allgemeinen" (1:17). This decision is, of course, one that is unexpected in the circles of the businessman and, as a matter of fact, is one with which many people take issue. Apparently it is not the outrageous notion of setting out to be a "general scientist" that upset those who express their criticism, but rather the lack of contribution to the bourgeois society. Heinrich's father defends the idea by stating that each person can only perform a duty to society by fulfilling himself: "Gegen diesen Einwurf sagte mein Vater, der Mensch sei nicht zuerst der menschlichen Gesellschaft wegen da sondern seiner selbst willen. Und wenn jeder seiner selbst willen auf die beste Art da sei, so sei er es auch für die menschliche Gesellschaft" (1:18). The father's thinking is economic in nature. Not only does he formulate ideas that coincide with the principles of the market economy, but his ideas also reverberate of David Ricardo's early nineteenth-century theory of comparative advantage. Considering economics, this theory says that if each nation specializes in the type of industrial production in which it is best, the total economic output can be optimized. This happens even though one nation might be better at several things. Similarly, as Heinrich's father points out, the benefit to society is optimized when each person's potential is developed to its fullest.

While Heinrich himself feels a certain undefined attraction to the idea of becoming a scientist, he acknowledges that he will not be able to learn all of the sciences:

> Das sah ich wohl troz meiner Jugend schon ein, daß ich nicht alle Wissenschaften würde erlernen können; aber was und wieviel ich lernen würde, das war mir eben so unbestimmt, als mein Gefühl unbestimmt war, welches mich zu diesen Dingen trieb. Mir schwebte auch nicht ein besonderer Nuzen vor, den ich durch mein Bestreben erreichen wollte, sondern es war mir nur, als müßte ich so thun, als liege etwas innerlich Gültiges und Wichtiges in der Zukunft (1:17–18).

The whole rationale, or rather, lack thereof, that supports Heinrich's choice of profession, goes not only against the pragmatism of the bourgeois economy, but also contradicts the father's focus on the devotion to and pursuit of just one thing. While it is easy to recognize the incongruence in the ideas of Heinrich's father, his behavior is mitigated by the fact that he is not simply a businessman but also a man with great aesthetic interests as well. He is devoted to sharing his knowledge of art and literature with his children when he describes in detail how the effects of color and light function in works of art: "Er zeigte uns, wenn wir spazieren gingen, die Wirkungen von Licht und Schatten, er nannte uns die Farben, welche sich an den Gegenständen befanden, und erklärte uns die Linien, welche Bewegung verursachten, in welcher Bewegung doch wieder eine Ruhe herrschte, und Ruhe in Bewegung sei die Bedingung eines jeden Kunstwerkes" (1:16). In his role as paterfamilias, as father and educator of his children, he imparts his profound aesthetic principles to his son and daughter.

Furthermore, there is a clear juxtaposition of the father's affinities for both, business and the fine arts. The following highlights his justification of integrating the two areas: "der Vater zeigte uns seine Bilder, und erklärte uns manches in denselben. Er sagte, daß er nur alte habe, die einen gewissen Werth besitzen, den man immer haben könne, wenn man einmal genöthigt sein sollte, die Bilder zu verkaufen" (1:16). The concept of selling his art is not foreign to him, and he clearly expresses the existence of a market value. In the world of the father there is an obvious transparency between the aesthetic and monetary aspects of the artifact. For Heinrich's father the appreciation of the works of art is not solely based on their *intrinsic* aesthetic value but, as the quote demonstrates, also on their *extrinsic* market value. It also shows that the market value of the pictures is reliable over time and not threatened by heavy market fluctuations. The pictures can always be sold at a certain price. As businessman the father acknowledges the financial reality of life and buys the art partly to protect himself and his family against "a rainy day".[5]

Heinrich's father also teaches him sound financial principles. When Heinrich and his sister inherit some money from a relative on their mother's side, the father invests it securely and adds the accrued annual interest to the assets. There is a certain progression in Heinrich's freedom as pertaining to his access to the capital. In the beginning, all the control is in his father's hands, but as Heinrich grows older, more and more of the responsibility is given to him. The father outlines how he will provide Heinrich with a certain amount of money every month, and it will be Heinrich's obligation to economize and do the bookkeeping (*Buch führen*) (1:25). This is indeed the "*Soll und Haben*" that defines the financial relationship between father and son. There is a clear expectation that Heinrich's bookkeeping must agree with that of the father. This insistence on the compatibility of the financial figures reinforces the notion of the prescribed and all-encompassing order of the father. Any digression from this patriarchal system is unacceptable.

When the father elaborates on the arrangements surrounding his financial agreement with Heinrich, he clarifies that there will be absolutely no cash advances of the allowance. Heinrich will have to economize appropriately and use only the money he has access to at any given moment. The concept of credit is unmistakably rejected. This stipulation against credit simultaneously safeguards against over-consumption. In addition, a non-negotiable price is established for

5 This attitude is different from the reigning principles at the Rosenhaus where the market forces are disregarded. Instead, only the inherent aesthetic value of art is the guiding principle of the price setting mechanism. These principles will be discussed further under the rubric of "The Fair Price and the Silence of the Market."

Heinrich's room and board in his father's house. It is expected that he will continue to live with his parents even though his financial situation, at least partially, has been separated from theirs.

At the same time as Heinrich's financial freedom increases, he also expands his world by embarking on educational journeys, which support his pursuits in achieving a certain level of expertise in different fields of science. Being separated from his parents gives Heinrich an urge for self-expression: "Weil ich mit den Meinigen nicht zusammenkommen konnte, so lebte die Sehnsucht nach Mittheilung viel stärker in mir, als wenn ich zu Hause gewesen wäre, und sie jeden Augenblick hätte befriedigen können" (1:28). Diligent practice equips him with improved skills in the "Gabe der Darstellung und Erzählung," so that he is able to conclude: "Ich schritt zu immer zusammengesezteren und geordneteren Schilderungen" (1:29). Heinrich's improvement in the realm of writing appears to be defined by his ability to organize and put his *Stoff* together to a unified whole.

In conjunction with this development of expressive tendencies in the protagonist, the *Ich-Erzähler* also makes reference to Heinrich's fascination with true representation: "Ich war schon als Knabe ein großer Freund der Wirklichkeit der Dinge gewesen [...] Ich fragte unaufhörlich um die Namen der Dinge um ihr Herkommen und ihren Gebrauch[...]. Auch konnte ich es nicht leiden, wenn man einen Gegenstand zu etwas Anderem machte, als er war" (1:29). Heinrich's insistence on accuracy between the object and its representation is an indication of his preference for realist representation.

Once Heinrich ventures forth from the somewhat restrictive environment of his parents' house, he encounters Freiherr von Risach, whose name remains a mystery throughout much of the story. The first time Heinrich comes upon the *Rosenhaus*, the most crucial place of his education, von Risach identifies himself simply as "der Herr des Hauses." With Heinrich's extended travels, which include annually repeated and extensive visits to the *Rosenhaus*, his concept of the family is altered. The encounter between Heinrich and von Risach marks the beginning of the gradual change from the traditional, sometimes confining, nuclear family to the expanded notion of the complementary circle of people at the *Rosenhaus*.[6] This change takes place in stages and starts with the encounter between Heinrich and Freiherr von Risach. It is von Risach who firmly occupies the center of the *Rosenhaus* community and who will become Heinrich's role model and principal In accordance with this monopolistic, paternal structure in the *Nachsommer*, the whole educational enterprise, as Hans Rindisbacher points out, is a one-way street where discourse is "authoritarian and always humbly, submissively received at the subordinate level" (Rindisbacher, 63).

For my interpretation I relate this principle of organization around a father figure – due to the absence of names it is really a symbolic construction in which everything revolves around the nameless father – which can be related to Jean-Joseph Goux's discussion of the general equivalent. The general equivalent is an economic concept; money is placed in an exclusive position as the measurement of the values of all other commodities. This is the quantitative aspect. Goux extends the theory of the general equivalent to other domains, "where values are no longer economic, where the play of substitutions defines qualitative values" (Goux, 3). Goux states: "In short, I came to affirm that the Father becomes the general equivalent of subjects, Language the general equivalent of signs, and the Phallus the general equivalent of objects, in a way that is structurally and genetically homologous to the accession of a unique element (let us say Gold, for the sake of simplicity) to the rank of the general equivalent of products" (4). Goux's concept of the general equivalent applies to the representational model of *Der Nachsommer*. The monopolistic notion of paternal rule in the *Nachsommer* narrative defines the whole educational enterprise in the novel. As exemplified in the father's demand for accurate bookkeeping, the standard of the father is the

6 Klaus-Detlef Müller (1971) draws attention to the fact that isolation is the guiding principle of Heinrich's education: "Entscheidend für die Erziehung ist das Prinzip der Isolierung: keine öffentliche Schule, kein gesellschaftlicher Umgang und nach dem Erwerb des Vorstadthauses auch keine räumliche Erweiterung durch Reisen mehr. Bildungsmächtig ist allein der enge Kreis der Familie, der ganz und gar durch den Willen des Vaters geformt ist" (124).

measure of everything, just as money has an institutionalized position of privileged representativeness in the money economy.[7]

The reigning principle of the father-centered environment in *Der Nachsommer* is agreement. The boundaries between traditionally conflicting spheres are diffused. Surely, questions are being asked, and many interesting conversations take place between the characters, but there is never really any substantive questioning of facts, ideas, or conclusions. This is partly a hierarchical and patriarchal tendency, i.e., the word of the father is the law, but it is also partly a development whereby the members of the younger generation, above all Heinrich, grow into deserving an increased measure of authority. This happens through a slow realization and appreciation of the Beautiful, where generational conflict is not part of the process of developing and growing up.[8]

7 Jean-Joseph Goux (1990) relates phallocentrism, logocentrism, and economic exchange to each other within the same framework, claiming that they are part of a unified process. He finds that value gathers, capitalizes, centralizes itself, giving some elements a privileged representativeness, and even a monopoly on representativeness. The reason why this process takes place is that one commodity rises up to a power position of a representative, and then this role becomes institutionalized. The connection among the three (phallocentrism, logocentrism, and economic exchange) makes it possible to define major social formations as "a mode of symbolizing that is both economic and significant" (4). The conclusion he draws is that the critique of money appears as the paradigm of a critique of a certain mode of symbolizing, whose philosophical aspect is idealism.

8 J.P. Stern discusses *Der Nachsommer* and its peculiar mode of Bildungsroman in his book *Idylls and Realities: Studies in Nineteenth-Century German Literature*. He concludes that Stifter transforms the genre because he departs from the focus on educational "process of becoming" (119). To the contrary, Stifter focuses on a "state of being" (119), "The journey is no longer more absorbing than its goal, simply because the journey is the goal: 'becoming' becomes being" and further "A state of finality replaces the provisional and experimental mode of the Bildungsroman..." (120). Stern's notion that *Der Nachsommer* digresses from the tradition of the Bildungsroman is interesting, but my own discussion of the novel uses a different conceptual framework and does not focus on genre issues. However, my argument concerning the lack of crystallization in Heinrich's personality parallels Stern's discussion of Stifter's departure from the "process of becoming." The point of my discussion of Heinrich's "development" is to show the inner workings of Stifter's economo-

I argue that Heinrich's very nature is that of a non-person. Due to the focus on the fatherly will that imbues the narrative, Heinrich's personality assimilates to the paternal ideal as he develops.[9] This tendency towards conformity is peculiar in light of the value of individuality preached by the voice of the father. As I pointed out earlier, Heinrich's father defends the profession of scientist as valuable because only by following one's calling (*Beruf*) can one fulfill oneself, and thereby perform a duty to society. Paradoxically, it seems that Heinrich reaches his peak of individuality at the moment when he becomes completely "conventional."

The insistence on individuality could be interpreted as a criticism of usefulness and efficiency, as well as the economic equivalent of these concepts, the money economy, where everything is exchangeable for money, and where everything has a price. While in such a system there is a clear loss of individuality of both objects and people, the narrative undermines its own (structural) criticism of money by not allowing Heinrich to crystallize his personality. On the contrary, Heinrich becomes more *like* money, i.e., able to engage with the world as a neutral medium of exchange, without adding his (absent) individuality to the outcome of the process. To say the least, the narrative is ambivalent in its attitude towards money's infinite possibilities of signification. There are other such discrepancies in the novel that I will discuss further later in this chapter.

---

poetics in *Der Nachsommer*, not to question the novel's place within the tradition of the Bildungsroman.

9 In his 1948 study of *Der Nachsommer*, Eric Blackall points out that Stifter's desire for abstraction is similar to that of Expressionist authors whom tended to use type-names in their dramatic works. Blackall identifies this tendency towards abstraction in the singular outlock on life which Stifter expresses in *Der Nachsommer*: "There is only one outlook on life in this book – that which Stifter conceived to be the ideal outlook. The only differentiation between the characters is that Risach and Mathilde have attained to this outlook, whereas Heinrich and Natalie are shown as developing towards it .... Heinrich is simply a Risach in development and Natalie stands in the same relation to Mathilde" (330). While Blackall certainly makes astute observations relating to *Der Nachsommer*, many of his arguments are used to affirm his own admiration of the novel and to speculate about Stifter's intentions.

Money, Consumption, and the Capitalist Economy

The major economic principle in *Der Nachsommer* is that of self-sustenance. This is of primary importance to my interpretation of Stifter's work because it reflects the poetic structure of the novel. In *Der Nachsommer*, the autarchic organization results in a state where the sphere of the economy seems to have disappeared. This marginalization of the material economy, though, is merely an illusion. In reality, the utopian existence of von Risach and his successor Heinrich relies on money. Stifter's sentimental utopia, which idealizes the past, attempts to exclude the new economic paradigm by implementing a pre-industrial economic system. For example, starting at an early age, Heinrich lives off of his inherited assets, receiving the interest from the money his father invested wisely. Only by means of bourgeois capital can Heinrich pursue his path towards an existence in the spirit of the Enlightenment, far from any industrial specialization. In this respect, autarchy is a mere illusion. The utopian world at von Risach's estate depends on the very economic structures Stifter omits.

Heinrich's father is as active a participant in the bourgeois capitalist economy in his capacity as a businessman, as Heinrich is removed from this world. This is not only because Heinrich is pursuing a career as a scientist, an occupation which does not directly generate capital, but also he is independently wealthy. An inheritance from a great-uncle enables him to abstain from involvement in the material economy. Thus, he can focus on gaining scientific knowledge, and in essence, accumulating his wealth of knowledge. He considers focusing on mathematics: "Man hatte mir immer gesagt, sie sei die schwerste und herrlichste Wissenschaft, sie sei die Grundlage zu allen übrigen, in ihr sei alles wahr, und was man aus ihr habe, sei ein bleibendes Besiztum für das ganze Leben" (Stifter, 1:27). The choice of words (*Besitztum*) demonstrates the influence of the underlying doctrine that governs the *Nachsommer* narrative. In this case, it is used in the discourse of education. In building his knowledge of mathematics, Heinrich expands his intellectual capital base and thereby ensures a basic foundation for further scientific competencies.

In spite of Heinrich's wealth, he does not devote it to corporeal consumption (other than the intangible "consumption" of books and equipment for his scientific pursuits). At times, the text is quite specific as to the kinds of things Heinrich purchases: "Ich kaufte mir die Bücher, die man mir rieth.... Ich kaufte mir eine sehr große Schiefertafel, um auf ihr meine Arbeiten ausführen zu können" (1:27). The text wants to ensure its readers that there is a reason for everything Heinrich acquires, more specifically, the purpose of his edification. In the realm of the material economy, any consumption for consumption's sake needs to be obliterated. All resources are to be devoted to the realm of aesthetics, and preferably to the aesthetics of the useful – projects that combine utility with aesthetic qualities.

When the time comes for Heinrich to control independently all the revenue that his assets yield, his father educates him in the art of investing. It is his opinion that Heinrich should not be greedy by trying to maximize the interest earned from his capital. On the contrary, he should avoid unnecessary financial risk and focus on minimizing his spending: "Sei immer deines Grundvermögens sicher, und mache die dadurch entstehende kleinere Rente durch Mäßigkeit größer" (1:35). In other words, Heinrich's father warns Heinrich about the dangers of financial risk, but he also advocates restraint in consumption. This kind of restraint is part of the Drendorf household. There is a certain simplicity to the lives of its members. On the very first page of the novel, for example, the *Ich-Erzähler* clarifies: "Wir Kinder bekamen einfache Speisen..." (1:9). He goes on to describe the clothing of the mother: "Zu Hause hatte sie gewöhnlich sehr einfache Kleider an." The beautiful antique jewelry the father owns is not meant for practical use, i.e., for wear, and "consumption," but only for "pure" aesthetic enjoyment: "Dabei fiel uns auf, daß sie immer ganz einfache obwohl sehr glänzende Steine hatte, und daß ihr der Vater nie die geschnittenen umhing, von denen er doch sagte, daß sie so schöne Gestalten in sich hätten" (1:12). This kind of simplicity continues at the *Rosenhaus*, Heinrich's home-away-from-home, where the meals are quite Spartan in nature: "Das Abendessen war sehr einfach" (1:80).

Stifter distinguishes the closed world of the *Rosenhaus* from the rest of society. Heinrich also begins to develop an interest is the world of precious stones. When Heinrich returns from one of his visits to the *Rosenhaus*, he discovers that there is ample opportunity in the city to view beautiful precious stones. The implication is that they are meant for consumption: "In unzähligen Schaufenstern der Stadt liegen Schmuckwerke zur Ansicht und zur Verlockung zum Kaufe aus" (1:90). Influenced by von Risach, Heinrich is more interested in the fashion in which the stones and metals are brought together to become jewelry. The more attuned to the classic ideals of simplicity these settings are, the more aesthetically appealing they will be.

Refraining from consumption is a strategy to avoid the support of an economy in which the abundance of products has become a temptation to the consumer. Increased consumption in society is a threat to fiscal stability because it exercises a pressure on money supply and allows for inflationary forces to come into play. Money supply and increased consumption follow and spiral upward together, and the principle of scarcity upon which money's function rests, becomes compromised.[10] This upward spiraling is therefore threatening to money's power in the process of signification. Inflation depletes the value of money and redefines its position as a medium of exchange.

Peter Pfeiffer describes this phenomenon of consumption restraint in *Der Nachsommer* by focusing on an excerpt from *Wien und die Wiener*, where Stifter elaborates on the changes in the process of exchange in a money-based economy. The changes involve a transformation from money as a mere facilitator in the process of exchange to becoming the common denominator of all things, and in effect, as Pfeiffer writes, the absolute sign that has subsumed all other signs. Pfeiffer continues: "In this changed environment, proper signification is no longer possible because the clear distinction between

10 Jochen Hörisch (1996) calls the phenomenon of compromised scarcity "de-substantialization" of money (197), which in turn he relates to the (previous) shift from "religious to monetary ontosemiology" (196). The subsequent development of audio-visual media around 1900 began to "erode the monetary medium" (197). Hörisch explains: "They overwrite not only the classical form of metal and paper money by turning money in to the form in which the sums that really count are handled. They also establish a second currency in societies [...] celebrities" (197).

the representation of 'things' and the things themselves has become obscured." This in turn, leads to an "ever-accelerating circulation of signifiers – of money – that simulates social relations and feeds a frenzy of consumption..." (Pfeiffer, 80–1). In a way then, rejecting consumption as part of the capitalist market economy is analogous to resisting money's potentially uncontrolled process of signification, and, by extension, to maintaining a stable representational structure between signifiers and signified – both in economic and literary-aesthetic terms. Pfeiffer's findings about consumption and its aesthetic implications in *Der Nachsommer* are relevant to my own discussion of the total economization which takes place in Stifter's text.

This withdrawal from the act of consumption and thereby from the arbitrary modes of representation in the paper money economy is only part of Stifter's critique of modern market forces. The almost exclusive focus on von Risach's world at the *Rosenhaus* is an implicit negation of budding industrialism and the economic phenomena that accompany it. Stifter does not address the state of the real, current economy. The *Nachsommer* environment can be labeled as a retrospective utopia of sorts because Stifter exclusively describes pre-industrial modes of existence and production. As a matter of fact, Stifter decided against using the originally planned subtitle *Eine Erzählung aus unseren Tagen* and instead focuses on a time around 1820–1825, and "schafft so eine künstliche, erhöhte Gegenwelt zu seiner realen Wirklichkeit, eine Gegenwelt, die trotz der Verankerung in sozio-ökonomischen Bedingungen einer bestimmten historischen Situation utopische Züge trägt" (Lachinger, 98).

The *Nachsommer* milieu can be accurately described as autarchy, at least in economic terms. Stifter constructs a closed economy at the *Rosenhaus* in which its members provide for all the needs that exist in their community. In addition to extensive farming activities, such as growing different grains and hay, and animal husbandry, there are greenhouses, fruit trees, vegetable gardens, and beehives, since everything necessary to sustain life is present at the *Rosenhaus*. Also, there are no textual references to participation in the economy as a whole; the produce and other products of the farm seem to be kept away from the general, external circulation of goods and money. Actually, the text makes reference to the fact that the farming is done for the purpose of providing for internal needs: "Als wir von der entgegengesezten Seite des Hauses fortgingen, sahen wir auch den Garten, in welchem die Gemüse und andere Dinge für den Gebrauch des Hofes gezogen wurden" (Stifter, 1:138).

The autarchic system that Stifter constructs in *Der Nachsommer* clearly enables the *Rosenhaus* to remain "uncontaminated" by outside market forces and tendencies towards overconsumption. In addition, the farming that takes place is not only utilitarian in nature but also combines a progressive sense of utility with aesthetic ideals: "Für die Rinder war hinter dem Hause ein schöner Plaz eingefangen, auf welchem sie in freie Luft gelassen werden konnten. Es strömte frisches Wasser in einer tiefen Steinrinne durch den Platz, von welchem sie trinken konnten. Ich hatte diese Einrichtung nie gesehen, und sie gefiel mir sehr" (1:137). As von Risach comments on the utilitarian – and at the same time aesthetically pleasing – systems and ideas that are being implemented at the farm, he alludes to the fact that things are progressing slowly because his workers are not quite ready to embrace these new ideas: "Man muß die Vorurtheile der Leute schonen, die unter anderen Umgebungen herangewachsen und sie gewohnt sind, damit sie nicht durch das Neue beirrt werden, und ihre Liebe zur Arbeit verlieren. Wir müssen uns beruhigen, daß schon so vieles geschehen ist, und auf das Weitere hoffen" (1:137–8).

The counterworld to the *Rosenhaus* autarchy, the capitalist economy, differs greatly from von Risach's utopian model. Stifter's creation of the closed economy at the *Rosenhaus* protects from the destructive habits of contemporary business practices. In his article "Patriarchalisches Stilleben? Ein sozialgeschichtlicher Versuch über Stifters Nachsommer," Karl Wagner describes the state of business in the mid 1800s.[11] He cites from the essay "Über unsere gegenwärtige

11 Wagner (1980) also makes reference to Thomas Carlyle's characterization of that era as the Mechanical Age in which machinery reins. Carlyle states: "It is the Age of the Machinery, in every outward and inward sense of that word; the age which, with its whole undivided might, forwards, teaches and practices the great art of adapting means to ends. Nothing is now done directly, or by hand; all is rule and calculated contrivance" (156). Especially this last sentence is interesting in relation to the representational capacity of money. Carlyle is describing a system that parallels the paper money economy. It is an economy

Lage" from 1849, in which Stifter laments the lack of *Geschäftsehre* in his contemporary society:

> Im Handel will man schnell reich werden, weil man die Sitten von Vornehmen darstellen will, weil man Aufwand machen, weil man glänzen will, weil man sich in dem schlechtesten aller Stolze zeigen will, in dem Stolze der Verschwendung. Wie schnell sieht man daher heutzutage in Hauptstädten Unternehmungen entstehen und zu Grunde gehen. Selbst die Lüge, die Übervorteilung, ja das Betrügen muß helfen, Geld herein zu bringen (GW, 6:343).[12]

Stifter's presentation of an aesthetically appealing, and at the same time functionally adequate, self-contained economic system constitutes a declaration of suspicion of the external market economy described above. The forces of the market economy instigate consumption, which, in turn, is the originator of a volatile and threatening system of signification and exchange, a system in which money flows freely and uncontrollably as it partakes in the process of commodity exchange. *Der Nachsommer* was published in a time of economic crisis and rapid price increases (Wagner, 162). Stifter's autarchic countermodel endorses a state whereby consumption takes place only in relation to the naturally existing need, not in relation to the man-made, and therefore artificial, want.

In spite of the fact that, on one level, the *Nachsommer* autarchy results in the disappearance of the larger market economy, on another level, this negation of the economy is an illusion because ultimately everything is economized. Some indicators of this are the reliance on interest from capital, the "productive" use of time, as well as the insistence on paying a fair price for artifacts. This tension between the apparent exclusion of the economic from the text and the simultaneous reliance on the very components that define it will be discussed in detail later in this chapter.

---

in which there is a loss of concrete relationships in the production chain and an increasing reliance on abstract thinking and calculation.

12 Stifter originally wrote this article for the *Wiener Bote* in 1849. It appears as one in a series of essays entitled *Über unsere gegenwärtige Lage und unsere sittliche Verbesserung* in Adalbert Stifter. *Gesammelte Werke*. Frankfurt: Inselverlag, 1959; hereafter referred to as GW.

Similarly to *Soll und Haben*, *Der Nachsommer* does not focus on industrial production. Quite the opposite, its basis is the pre-industrial society in which the tradition of *Handwerk* is still predominant, at least within the realm of the autarchy of the *Rosenhaus*. Von Risach is very critical of the new money economy[13], glorifying the "good old days" when the farm workers were dependents of the big household and bemoaning the demise of the paterfamilias: He states: "Seit sie aber von ihm getrennt sind, für die Arbeit bezahlt werden und abgesondert ihre Nahrung erhalten, gehören sie nicht zu ihm nicht zu seinem Kinde, haben andere Zwecke, widerstreben ihm, verlassen ihn leicht..." (Stifter, 1:135–6).

Heinrich, on the other hand, exhibits a certain measure of curiosity in the processes that are being used in nearby factories, but his way of examining their inner workings is that of a scientist:

> Ich besuchte nach und nach alle diese Fabriken, und unterrichtete mich über die Erzeugnisse, welche da hervorgebracht wurden. Ich suchte den Hergang kennen zu lernen, durch welchen der Stoff in die Fabrik geliefert wurde, durch welchen er in die erste Umwandlung, von dieser in die zweite und so durch alle Stufen geführt wurde, bis er als leztes Erzeugniß der Fabrik hervorging (1:31).

Heinrich wants to understand the transformations, the translations, if you will, that take place within the walls of the factory. He scientifically dissects the production process and then attempts to gain a more holistic understanding of industrial production: "Ich ging

13 In her study of the meaning and function of interiors in *Der Nachsommer*, Kirsten Belgum focuses on the novel's project of aesthetic restoration which she relates to the "social restoration of the bourgeois family" of the mid-century (15). The concept of the "whole house" (15–16) – the site of economic production and the foundation of morality and social stability – is part of this restoration project. Belgum views the interior of the Rosenhaus as an expression of these ideals: "The interior of this perfect home serves as the well-ordered center for the family and reinforces all the qualities – hierarchy, tastefulness, beauty, and unmarred totality – that the family should possess" (16).

durch die Gefälligkeit der dabei Angestellten alle Theile durch, bis ich das Ganze so vor mir hatte, und zusammen begreifen konnte, als hätte ich es als Zeichnung auf dem Papier liegen, wie ich ja bisher alle Einrichtungen solcher Art nur aus Zeichnungen kennen zu lernen Gelegenheit hatte" (1:31). Just as in his scientific endeavors, Heinrich uses the visual mode to mediate reality and transform it into an understandable and more complete concept by drawing everything he observes.

Heinrich is not the only character in *Der Nachsommer* to operate externally to industrial society. As a matter of fact, none of the other main characters are involved with the capitalist production of goods. They engage in activities such as the replication and restoration of artifacts. These activities, though always performed with great skill and effectiveness, cannot be categorized as productive work in a capitalist sense because they do not generate profits for those involved, something that would be expected of capitalist production. Instead, the purpose of their endeavors in the production of "aesthetic surplus" falls mainly within the realm of categorizing, cataloguing, and systematizing the objects they work with.

While the pieces of furniture (*Geräthe*) reproduced at the *Asperhof* are built with a strong sense of antiquity, they are simultaneously products of the current time with elements of the past. This relationship to the aesthetic ideals of the past points to the aesthetic integrity that is so important to the message the novel delivers: "Die Gestalten der Geräthe sind nach der Art entworfen worden, die wir vom Alterthume lernten, wie ich euch einmal sagte, aber so daß wir nicht das Alterthum geradezu nachahmten, sondern selbständige Gegenstände für die jetzige Zeit verfertigten mit Spuren des Lernens an vergangenen Zeiten" (1:294).

Further, von Risach emphasizes that it is imperative not to deceive, but to be explicit instead with the heritage of each piece: "Damit aber niemand irre geführt werde, ist jedem solchen altneuen Stücke ein Silberplättchen eingefügt, auf welchem die Thatsache in

Buchstaben eingegraben ist" (1:298). This is a way of authenticating those pieces of art that are of *Neuproduktion.*[14]

The other main preoccupation of the characters in *Der Nachsommer* is the organization and *Bändigung* of nature into preferred shapes and forms – ultimately, the desire to control nature. As von Risach establishes himself at the *Asperhof*, he goes to great lengths to aestheticize the garden. He even orders the moving of big, full-grown trees to accomplish a certain aesthetic effect. As the trees were replanted in their assigned places in the new garden area surrounding the *Asperhof*, incredible measures were taken to ensure their survival and thriving. Von Risach had gigantic holes dug so that the roots of the trees would not have to break into new, untilled ground for a long time. Also, the subsequent care of the trees goes beyond the expected and reasonable: "Im Frühlinge wird jeder Stamm und seine stärkeren Äste durch eine Bürste und gutes Seifenwasser gewaschen und gereinigt" (1:150). This ultimate standard of care, which von Risach provides for the objects and creatures in his immediate environment, is completely futile in the sense of productiveness. The futility lies in the fact that the goal of the rearrangements in the *Asperhof* garden is to make it look natural: "In kürzerer Zeit, als man glauben sollte, hatten wir die Freude, zu sehen, daß der Garten so zusammengewachsen erschien, als wäre er nie an einem andern Plaze gewesen" (1:129). From a pragmatic standpoint, one would have to ask, "What is the point? Why recreate something that was perfectly composed by nature to begin with?" This molding and reshaping of nature parallels the process of literary production in the realm of Poetic Realism. While the urge to create a "natural" and true depiction of reality is at

14 Belgum also points to the apparent lack of authenticity at the time: "By 1850 the pluralism of styles in arts and crafts production had become so inclusive that many critics attacked it for being undirected or lacking a sense of taste altogether" (17). Risach's insistence on harmonizing objects and reproducing the pieces that are causing deficiencies in the totality of his collections can be interpreted as part of this general sentiment. The process of creating perfectly seamless and historically correct interiors is mirrored in the narrative structure of the novel. Stifter's language "ensures that no gaps are left for self-interpretation by the reader; ideas and actions are expressed in excessive completeness so that no space remains for disruption" (21).

the center of this literary style, just as in the case of von Risach's garden, the result of this literary creation of a fictitious reality is clearly different from the original in spite of striving to stay true to its nature. The interesting thing is, of course, that in *Der Nachsommer* the reworking of nature into a different and much refined "natural" state is preferred over the original, untouched nature. When von Risach and some members of the Rosenhaus discuss a further rearrangement of the trees in order to achieve a stronger color effect, they decide against such a measure because: "eine zu ängstliche Zusammenstellung der Farben verrathe die Absicht und störe die Wirkung; eine reizende Zufälligkeit sei doch das Angenehmste" (1:259). This decision underscores the fact that it is desirable to avoid any recreation of nature that reveals the intent of the mimesis or that leads to an unnatural sense of orderliness in the arrangement of the display.

With regard to the topic of "production," the conclusion is clearly that the creation of a complete unit of aesthetic (man-made) naturalness, as the *Asperhof* exemplifies, is seen as much more valuable than participation in the capitalist economy. In addition, the extrapolation of the notions discussed above points to the idea that the fictitious reality of the literary text is preferred over reality itself.

The *Asperhof* rose garden is another example of how achieving a certain aesthetic effect is more important than following the lead of nature. These roses are grown against the forces of nature because a memory from von Risach's youth makes it appealing to him to grow the roses along the southern wall of the house. Heinrich does not understand how the roses can possibly thrive the way they are grown at the *Asperhof*: "Sie haben hier eigentlich die ungünstigsten Bedingungen. Da ist das hölzerne Gitter, an das sie mit Zwang gebunden sind, die weiße Wand, an der sich die brennenden Sonnenstrahlen fangen..." (1:143). For each of the problems that Heinrich lists, von Risach offers a detailed description of a system he has invented to overcome the hurdles inherent in the placement of the roses along that particular wall. He has special irrigation, ventilation, and sun protection systems for his treasured roses. This way of working against nature in order to achieve a desired effect is a common theme in *Der Nachsommer*. When it comes to the roses, the desired effect includes the kind of perfection that does not allow for any old, unhealthy, or otherwise impaired roses. It is a sanitized world deprived of imperfection. The non-exemplary samples are quickly taken to a special *Rosenhospital* and replaced by healthy specimen so that the sick plants cannot contaminate the healthy ones "weil sie schon in der Zeit des Absterbens weggethan werden" (1:146).

In his book, *The Smell of Books: A Cultural-Historical Study of Olfactory Perception in Literature*, Hans Rindisbacher argues that smells are suppressed from the *Nachsommer* narrative. As a substitute for smells, there is a pronounced preference for the visual over all other senses. For example, he interprets the prevalence of marble in emotional situations as an indication that the cold, dead substance of marble has taken over the role traditionally attributed to the exuberant roses. Rindisbacher sees this as "sanitation" and as part of the representational structure of the novel. According to Rindisbacher, on the thematic level there is a clear lesson about the nature of mimesis, about coinciding representational forms of the visual and literary arts. Rindisbacher's explanation for the preferred position of the visual as the primary sense in *Der Nachsommer* is that visual objects can generally be collected and studied while there is an absence of educational possibility in the field of smells. Smells, being less tangible, have limited capacity to be collected or exhibited. "They lack all potential of forming social tradition" (Rindisbacher, 66). This point is exemplified by discussing the representation of the roses in *Der Nachsommer* and how the exclusion of smells bespeaks the aesthetic program of the text; the rose collection, in spite of the fact that the roses are viewed mostly as horticultural objects, is reduced to a visual presence. Thus by excluding the olfactory aspect of the roses, Stifter undermines the credibility of these flowers by making their sensory aspect less "holistic" because not all the senses crucial to fully experience roses are admitted. This idea is consistent with Risach's strategy to "sanitize" the natural world around him in his efforts to create a scenery that is even more pleasing aesthetically than the original.

Rindisbacher continues by claiming that the roses surrounding the *Asperhof* are growing on literary rather than actual soil; their reference to something other than themselves is not a semiotic one (as signifier standing for a signified) but rather symbolic: "They are not the roses accounting for the splendor of a summer garden. Their roots are in literary tradition, in poetry, romance, and the novel. This is the environment they point to and only here are they real. They grow as symbols and are paper roses from the start..." (67). This gap in the reference structure, as Rindisbacher claims, is filled with another material – marble – which becomes the preferred vehicle for the expression of feelings: (68) "Odorless stones, not scented roses, are the environment for the highest emotion" (71). The increasingly symbolic nature of representation in *Der Nachsommer* as exemplified in Rindisbacher's discussion of Stifter narrative distance, from the sensual fullness of the roses to the sanitized expression of marble, is part of a greater shift in representational practices. This shift equates the move to an abstract paper money economy. Paper money, like marble, is "cleaner" when embodying value because it is not contaminated by the substance it stands for – it solely represents.

During the course of his scientific pursuits Heinrich learns how to gather, organize, categorize, and reproduce materials from nature. This establishes the foundation of his aesthetic appreciation and capability. Likewise, the principle of natural laws seems to intrude into the sphere of aesthetics.[15] Just as the law of science remains unquestioned, there is an absence of argument about art. The aesthetic value of an object is transparent to those who possess the requisite insight. Another parallel between art and science is the idea that neither is connected with a passionate, innovative mind. The focus on learning craftsmanship suggests that any act of mimesis demands not so much creative ingenuity as a solid, refined mind and technically developed skills in the area of artistic production. Heinrich's

15 Eric Blackall has focused on these tendencies in his writings about *Der Nachsommer*. He claims that this novel is a different kind of Entwicklungsroman, one without struggle and conflict, and one in which art and science synthesize. In contrast to my own investigation, Blackall uses his findings to convince us of the superiority of *Der Nachsommer* within Stifter's body of work: "Art, Science, Ethics are merely individual aspects of the fundamental movement of the human soul towards God, the longing for order, peace and fulfillment. This is why *Der Nachsommer* transcends all Stifter's other works" (313).

developing sense for art and artistic reproduction evolves out of his scientific appreciation for and knowledge about the system of nature.

As Heinrich researches plants, he writes descriptions of those plants he cannot bring with him, such as trees. In the process, he realizes that the traditional categorization of plants is incomplete because it only categorizes according to one specific feature. Heinrich develops his own system, but he also keeps the traditional system: "Ich behielt die herkömmlichen Eintheilungen bei, und hatte aber auch meine Beschreibungen daneben" (Stifter, 1:32). Heinrich's descriptions do not imply a revolt against the existing system. To the contrary, they are a complement that ensures a fuller understanding of scientific reality. Heinrich goes on to do the same thing with minerals.

The close connection between art and science is evident also in Heinrich's father's view of possible professional prospects for his son: "Der Vater pflegte zu sagen, ich müßte einmal ein Beschreiber der Dinge werden, oder ein Künstler, welcher aus Stoffen Gegenstände fertigt, an denen er so Antheil nimmt, oder wenigstens ein Gelehrter, der die Merkmale und Beschaffenheiten der Sachen erforscht" (1:30). As Heinrich pursues his educational path he seems to devote some effort to all of these venues, even though, obviously, his scientific vein is the strongest. In his scientific work he definitely gains insight from perfecting his drawings of the plants and minerals that he is exploring.

In *Reflections of Realism: Paradox, Norm and Ideology in Nineteenth-Century German Prose*, Robert Holub discusses how Heinrich's pursuits in the sciences relate to art and realist representation. The process Heinrich goes through closely relates to the imagery of absolute beauty and Princess Nausikaa. Holub argues that in *Der Nachsommer*, the Nausikaa episode is a "prelude to two compositional features, one a reflection or self-reflection, the other the introduction of narrative device" (Holub, 62). Heinrich meets his own version of Nausikaa at a pivotal point in his development. As Holub suggests, Heinrich's Nausikaa encounter constitutes a reflection on realism in art; on the relationship of model to original. In *Der Nachsommer*, Nausikaa is connected with von Risach's marble statue from Cumae, which is in turn associated with Natalie. The relevance of Heinrich's encounter with the marble statue revolves around his progression to self-realization. In the initial stages of his friendship with von Risach, Heinrich's principal interests lie within the sphere of the natural sciences, even though he shows some affinity toward the arts. There is some indication of Heinrich's fluid movement between the sciences and the arts in his need to venture away from the restrictive classifications that are common in the sciences. Holub attributes this dissatisfaction to Heinrich's need for a more holistic perspective: "In cataloging minerals and plants, he mentions his dissatisfaction with the customary classifications: the scientific system orders things according to one of several characteristics; Heinrich prefers to retain along with this a classification based on overall perception and description" (67). The turning point away from a concentration on detail and on the separate parts of a whole towards a realization of the beauty of the whole occurs when Heinrich is confronted with the marble statue. The step from science to art appears to be marginal because, as Holub clarifies, "The function of both science and art is to give a true and precise picture or copy of the real world, and this mimetic relationship between artwork and reality is also coded into the Nausikaa episodes" (71). The marble statue only achieves artistic perfection when it becomes identified with Natalie. This final merger of art and reality completes Heinrich's educational process.

The Accumulation of Wealth and Collecting

A collection is an accumulation of both economic and aesthetic value. Collecting is a habit that requires a certain monetary surplus in the household economy. This surplus can be directed towards consumption or investment – the collecting of artifacts is one possible investment venue. The habit of collecting is specific to the expanding bourgeoisie during the nineteenth century, and it is partly a manifestation of its increased financial capabilities.[16] The principle of collecting permeates different arenas of society. In a discussion with Heinrich, von Risach points out that collecting is the current stage of scientific research: "Ich glaube, [...] daß in der gegenwärtigen Zeit der Standpunkt der Wissenschaft, von welcher wir sprechen, der des Sammelns ist" (Stifter 1:126–7). Scientific research, then again, is not the only sphere in which collecting is relevant. As Cornelia Blasberg demonstrates, there is a whole ideology of collecting and archiving in the nineteenth century to which *Der Nachsommer* belongs.[17]

The activity of collecting is portrayed as meaningful and desirable in the *Nachsommer* narrative. It is conducted with a certain measure of passion, particularly when it is part of striving for completion. This *Komplettierungsdrang* drives many of the choices and preferences of the characters in the novel. The habit of collecting objects is never viewed as anything but an esoteric, aesthetic, and harmless practice which serves the purpose of protecting the arts. The danger of collecting, the endless, and potentially out-of-control, striving for completion at any cost, never becomes an issue.

In her book, *Adalbert Stifter's Late Prose: The Mania for Moderation*, Helena Ragg-Kirby devotes one chapter to what she labels "Rituals and Sublimations." The main focus of this chapter is the phenomenon of collecting. The habit of collecting was not foreign to Stifter or to his contemporary society. As Ragg-Kirby points out,

16 According to David Blackbourn (1998), specifically the 1850s and 1860s were boom years in the growing industrial German nation, a boom that was only interrupted by the worldwide commercial and financial crisis in 1857.

17 C. Blasberg (1998), 114. Blasberg contends that the activity of collecting has two opposing aspects. On the one hand it has a connotation of concentration and calm as in the usage of the expression sich sammeln. On the other hand, there is what Blasberg describes as the "flüchtig-nervösen, akkumulations-begierigen, buchstäblich zerstreuten Sammler(s)". She explains further: "Der Reiz des einen schönen Gegenstandes führt ihn sogleich zum nächsten, der wiederum regt das Verlangen nach ähnlichen Objekten an" (122). According to Blasberg, the attraction of fragments is prevalent in *Der Nachsommer*, and is best exemplified by Heinrich's search for the missing Wandvertäfelungen. Risach's collection of different kinds of woods, on the other hand, is an example of konservierendes Sammeln that requires Töten and Zerstückeln (122).

Stifter situates himself and his own "Sammelgeist" in the tradition of collecting that he traces back to the legacy of Schiller and Goethe, Herder, and Kant: "Not only does Stifter suggest that he himself is endowed with the virtues of solidity and stability enshrined in this 'Sammelgeist': he also appears to attribute a similar immutability to his seemingly exemplary characters..." (Ragg-Kirby, 15). Von Risach in *Der Nachsommer* is, of course, one of these avid collectors. One of the things that Ragg-Kirby points out is that, in an effort to evade the human domain, the collections mainly focus on inanimate objects, including plants, minerals, and wood. This in turn creates a sense of objectivity: "On the face of it, these objects appear to have an unproblematic, reliable existence for Stifter, and therefore seem to function as bastions of security and meaning that afford protection against the beguiling pyrotechnics of human passions." Ragg-Kirby also contends that Heinrich is preoccupied with collecting data for his scientific research. In this capacity the "collection" serves as a way of controlling the forces of nature through the knowledge that it provides (16). In conclusion, some of these collecting activities, for example those connected with von Risach's roses, tend to go beyond that "innocent" endeavor to control nature. They develop into a "mania for trimming, training and controlling nature's inherent rampancy" (29). Ragg-Kirby interprets some of the most fervent collecting activities as both symbols and projections of oppressed sexuality.

Von Risach and Mathilde, jointly and separately, devote much attention to their collections. Within Ragg-Kirby's framework one could interpret their passionate collecting as a realm that protects against "real life" because they substitute their once passionate love for each other with collecting activities. This is especially true for von Risach whose entire rose collection is a reminder of his passion for Mathilde. Towards the end of the novel, when von Risach describes the nature of his relationship with Mathilde and her family to Heinrich, he points out how interconnected their lives are. Both von Risach and Mathilde are deeply involved in the restoration and collecting activities at the *Asperhof* and also the *Sternenhof*. Even though their present relationship is devoid of passion, they still possess both "Glück und Stettigkeit." As von Risach puts it, they live a "Nachsommer ohne vorhergegangenen Sommer." Part of this Indian summer that von Risach is alluding to is the process of completing his collection, a process analogous to fulfilling his life, to maturation: "Meine Sammlungen vervollständigen sich, die Baulichkeiten runden sich immer mehr..." (Stifter, 3:224).

This obsession with completion is also evident in von Risach's collection of special works of art and aesthetically pleasing buildings: "Diese Zeichnungen sind lauter Abbildungen von wirklichen Bauwerken, die in unserem Lande vorhanden sind[...]. Wir haben sie nach und nach zusammengebracht. Kein einziges Bauwerk unseres Landes, welches entweder im Ganzen schön ist, oder an dem Theile schön sind, fehlt" (1:105). The same ideas reign in the world of the roses:

> Das Haus war über und über mit Rosen bedeckt[...]. Es waren zudem fast alle Rosengattungen da, die ich kannte, und einige, die ich noch nicht kannte[...]. Die Pflanzen waren nicht etwa nach Farben eingetheilt, sondern die Rücksicht der Anpflanzung schien nur die zu sein, daß in der Rosenwand keine Unterbrechung stattfinden möge (1:47–8).

Just as in the case of the artwork, there is a clear striving for completion. In a matter of fact, aesthetic considerations in the arrangement of the roses are subordinate to the idea of completion.

When von Risach describes the origins of his art collection, he points out that it has been a continual process to achieve the aesthetic coverage it now exhibits: "Sie sind recht nach und nach in das Haus gekommen, wie es der Sammelfleiß und mitunter auch der Zufall gefügt hat[...]. Ich habe stets nach Bildern gesucht, habe Manches gekauft, Manches wieder verkauft, Neues gekauft, und so war ein fortlaufender Wechsel, bis es so wurde, wie es jezt ist" (2:102). According to von Risach's explanation there was a lively exchange of artworks before the collection eventually progressed into a state of completion and perfection. The focus on exchange (*Wechsel*) bespeaks the proximity of von Risach's collecting activities to financial transactions. In essence he is using the paintings as currency in the process of achieving perfection. In spite of this constant exchange, however, the controlled collection of aesthetically and financially valuable items is a restricted, almost static, expansion. It is static because, once the type of collectible has been selected, the "direction" of the collection has been determined, and only the potentially eternal expansion in that same direction will be pursued.

On some level, the activities connected with the different collections, from the acquisition to the restoration and eventual cataloguing of the individual pieces, are the essence of work; they contitute the creation of meaning. The extent to which one person was involved in the whole process is extremely important as von Risach tells Heinrich: "Ich habe meine Marmore alle selber in den Gebirgen gesammelt, und habe ihren Bruch aus den Felsen ihr Absägen, ihr Schleifen und ihre Einfügungen geleitet. Die Arbeit hat mir manche Freude gebracht, und ich glaube, daß mir nur darum diese Steine so lieb sind, weil ich sie selber gesucht habe." In fact, von Risach is reluctant to receive any marble specimens that originate from another person: "Da ich allen Marmor selber gesammelt habe, so kann ich wohl auch kein Stück an meinem Hause anbringen, das mir von fremder Hand käme" (1:127). This reluctance is an affirmation of von Risach's individuality.[18] It is also a reflection of the idea of perfection, i.e., where nothing can be "off"; that harmony, balance, and conformity are very important principles which must not be compromised.

These somewhat peculiar arguments are reiterated at a later stage when Mathilde wants to give her Goethe collection to her son, Gustav.

18 In his article, "The Museal Path to Bildung: Collecting, Exhibiting and Exchange in Stifter's *Der Nachsommer*," Peter McIsaac (2004) argues that von Risach's view of his marble collections as representations of his own personal history is part of the concept of Bildung in *Der Nachsommer*. By pursuing collection activities, Heinrich learns that his pursuits in this arena are directly related to the "cultivation and expression of identity" (275). In fact, McIsaac suggests "We can think of the construction of identity in this novel as involving an appropriation of available objects, rearranging the appealing parts, and quietly discarding those elements that are unsightly or unacceptable" (276). One important aspect that McIsaac adds to the notion of collecting in *Der Nachsommer* is the homosocial element of sharing the experience of collecting between the male protagonists. The experience of exhibiting the collection to the public is crucial to validate the worth of its originator. McIsaac employs a theoretical approach, the museum function, which he defines as "the way objects are valorised, acquired, and discarded, organised, displayed, and hidden in a particular society and historical period" (269).

He is moved but objects: “Aber siehst du, Mutter, da sind manche Zeilen mit einem feinen Bleistifte unterstrichen, und mit demselben feingespizten Stifte sind Worte an den Rand geschrieben, die von deiner Hand sind. Diese Dinge sind dein Eigenthum, sie sind in den neugekauften Büchern nicht enthalten, und ich darf dir dein Eigenthum nicht entziehen” (1:249–50). Mathilde’s Goethe collection is apparently different from other collections because it is inscribed with her own comments. In the process of reading the works, Mathilde has put her mark on the books by making notes and remarks that are intrinsically her own. Hence they differ in nature from new books. Again, the collection is an affirmation of individuality.

This repeated insistence on the individuality of collections is at the same time a resistance against capitalist consumer society in which every commodity has a price. In that system it does not matter who produced the object. In essence, all objects within that system are devoid of individuality. They are only defined in terms of their participation in the chain of commodity exchange. The topic of individuality also correlates directly to money because it was modern money, and specifically paper money, that gave rise to a system defined by symbolic representation. As the substance of money lost its meaning, money also lost its individuality, its aesthetic value, and thereby its value as a collectible.

This distancing from the modern economy is a theme that returns in *Der Nachsommer*. A pattern becomes apparent where in the midst of the retraction into a contained, deeconomized existence; there is still a reliance on the structures of the modern economy. This reliance on economics, in turn, compromises the criticism of those very economic structures. In regards to collections the compromise is twofold. First, the element of active exchange defines von Risach’s collecting activities. Second, the purpose of collecting is the accumulation of economic value. Even though the *Nachsommer* narrative mainly focuses on the purely aesthetic aspects of collecting, a collection always consists of a number of individual pieces, whose whole will be greater than the sum of its pieces (both aesthetically and financially). Consequently, the value of the collection exceeds that of the aggregate value of the individual pieces.

As Peter Pfeiffer shows in his essay, "Adalbert Stifter's Money Thing," capital accumulation is cast analogously to the accumulation of aesthetic value. This accumulation of aesthetic value is equivalent to the collection. Clearly, though, much effort is put into transferring the collection "into a semiotic system of readable signs, creating order, 'unzweideutige Zeichen' and certain meaning." The documentation of the collection "inscribes the essence of the 'Sammlung' into the book or ledger that keeps and exact and readable account of the accumulated aesthetic values and their meaning in the collection." The devotion to collections is also a means of directing attention and resources away from consumption: "The reduced level of material consumption as a way of life for Heinrich, his family, and Risach's circle allows a concomitant investment in aesthetic capital through restoration and documentation. This investment guarantees an ever-increasing richness and differentiation of meaning – and supports and increasing level of aesthetic consumption" (Pfeiffer, 84). Pfeiffer's reading of the collection activities in *Der Nachsommer* as a safeguard against consumption correlates with the idea presented above about the insistence on individuality as a venue for criticism of the capitalist economy.

Like von Risach, Heinrich's father is an avid collector of aesthetic objects. He owns precious stones and art. His collection of stones is actually quite impressive. Due to financial constraints, he was unable to start a broad-based collection including all the different manifestations of precious cuts. Instead of complete general coverage, he focuses on complete coverage in a subcategory:

> Ich bin nicht reich genug, eine große Sammlung von geschnittenen Steinen anlegen zu können, in welcher alle Gattungen enthalten sind, so fern man überhaupt Gelegenheit hat, sie zu kaufen, und weil ich das nicht konnte, so habe ich mich lediglich auf menschliche Gestalten beschränkt, und unter diesen wieder auf jene, deren Erwerb mir ohne Einfluß auf mein Hauswesen möglich war... (Stifter 2: 157).

This statement highlights two points. First, it reinforces the importance of "controlled" collecting, the notion that it is acceptable to channel money into a collection only with a financial surplus in the household economy. At no point is it admissible to compromise the financial equilibrium of the private economy in order to accumulate collectibles. The abstinence from financially "unwarranted" collecting, becomes an exercise in self-control. This leads to the second point. Heinrich's father resists the temptation to diffuse his collection by consistently limiting himself to a subcategory instead. Thereby the sum total of the collection holds a greater value than it would have, had it been broader in scope, but incomplete. Therefore, Drendorf's collecting behavior also teaches a certain investment economization because he is able to maximize the aesthetic and financial value for the money he spends.

Drendorf's collection has actually brought him joy in those moments when he had had feelings of apathy:

> Diese Steine sind durch viele Jahre mein Vergnügen gewesen. Oft in trüben Stunden, wenn Sorgen und Zweifel das Leben seines Duftes beraubten, und es dürr vor mich hinzubreiten schienen, bin ich zu dieser Sammlung gegangen, habe diese Gestalten angeschaut, bin in eine andere Zeit und in eine andere Welt versezt worden und bin ein anderer Mensch geworden (2:160).

The aesthetic value of the collection has transformational, perhaps even healing, powers, implying that it provides a way to escape from the constrictions and hardships of daily life.

The Fair Price and the Silence of the Market

As suggested above, the autarchy of the *Asperhof* does not engage in transactions in the general marketplace of goods and services. It distances itself from for-profit production and in its place focuses on self-sustenance and judges "unnecessary" consumption harshly. Quite analogously, transactions that are conducted in the realm of artifacts are sheltered from market influences. Those transactions are carried out based on a "fair-price" principle. The fair price relies entirely on an aesthetic evaluation of the artifact in question. For example, von Risach has accumulated a whole group of paintings intended for circulation, a "Vorrath zum Tausche" (2:102). He exchanges these newer paintings of lesser value for older, more valuable paintings. Von Risach often purchases paintings from those who are either ignorant or do not have the aesthetic finesse he himself possesses. However, at no time does von Risach make an effort to profit from this knowledge by buying the paintings at an unfairly low price. In other words, his exchange activities do not develop into a "business." To do so would be to succumb to the forces of the market economy. Instead, he always tries to compensate for the lesser value of his own paintings as he proceeds with the exchanges. As it turns out, the other people involved are usually satisfied with an even exchange. Whenever von Risach points out that their paintings are of greater value, and then declares himself ready to compensate for this discrepancy, the exchange partners understandibly are even happier: "Dieser macht ihnen Freude, und wenn ich ihnen darlegte, daß ihr Gemälde einen höheren Werth habe als das meinige, und wenn ich diesen Werth nach genauer Schätzung durch Geld ausglich, so war das Vergnügen noch größer..." (2:103).

As Pfeiffer points out: "Monetary value is envisioned to be determined not by the use-value of objects, through market forces, or the social labour invested in them (as Marx would have it). Rather, it is determined by what is deemed an objective aesthetic value. Aesthetic and monetary values are thought of as transparent and exactly equivalent" (Pfeiffer, 83). This negation of a price established by market forces reifies art and makes it a commodity. The marginalization of the market economy in *Der Nachsommer* is part of the principle of total economization that is critical to my reading of the novel's economopoetics. In spite of Stifter's attempts to exclude the market from the *Nachsommer* narrative, he cannot bypass the economic completely, and, on some level, his insistence on a fair price principle for artifacts results in the commodification of art.

As noted above, von Risach willingly participates in the circulation and exchange of paintings, yet makes it redundant because his aversion towards market forces becomes evident as soon as the true value of one of his purchases is revealed. At several instances in the novel, the modification of an already paid price occurs. For example, there is one particular painting, a *Marienbild*, which Roland finds by coincidence and subsequently purchases for von Risach. The text describes in detail how the painting had been mishandled by its former owners, and how von Risach's team restores it to its original glory. After lengthy discussions it is concluded that the painting was created by an Italian master. When the true origin and value of the painting are affirmed von Risach insists on compensating the former owner accordingly: "Dem Manne, von welchem das Bild in seinem verstümmelten Zustande gekauft worden war, gab ich noch eine Summe, mit welcher er weit über seine Erwartungen abgefunden war..." (Stifter, 2:110).

A similar situation occurs with the exquisite marble statue, which is given such a prominent place in von Risach house. When it is discovered that the statue is from ancient Greece and is not just a cheap plaster replica, von Risach travels to Italy to find the seller of the statue: "Ich erzählte ihm von der Entdeckung, welche ich gemacht hatte, und sagte, er möge nun nach derselben den Preis des Bildes bestimmen." Von Risach goes on to suggest that either the seller or his representative travel to Austria to inspect the statue to establish a fair price. Ultimately, the seller does not take him up on the offer: "Er fand beides nicht für nöthig, sondern forderte sogleich eine ansehnliche Summe, die den Werth eines solchen Gegenstandes, deren Preise in den verschiedenen Zeiten sehr wechseln, darstellen mochte" (2:83). Von Risach then proceeds to formalize the transaction by having a new contract drawn up that establishes the new "value" of the artifact: "Nachdem ich mir noch einen Kaufvertrag über das Marmorbild von einem Notar hatte verfassen lassen, und mich mit einer gefertigten Abschrift versehen hatte, erlegte ich die geforderte Summe, und reiste wieder nach Hause" (2:84).

At a later point, there is a peculiar incident with a collection of etchings (*Kupferstiche*) that are offered for sale. The members of the *Rosenhaus* circle decide:

> daß man der guten Stücke willen die ganze Sammlung kaufen wolle, wenn ihr Preis einen gewissen Betrag, den man anboth, und den man gerechter und billiger Weise geben konnte, nicht überstiege. Die schlechten Blätter wollte man dann vernichten, weil sie durch ihr Dasein eine gute Wirkung nicht nur nicht hervorvorbringen, sondern das Gefühl dessen, der nichts Besseres sieht,

statt es zu heben, in eine rohere und verbildetere Richtung lenken, als es nähme, wenn ihm nichts als die Gegenstände der Natur gebothen würden (3:132).

For this particular collection, von Risach is willing to pay a fair price even though some of its pieces are of mediocre quality. These pieces will be destroyed to avoid the "contamination" of the remaining pieces of the collection. In this instance, von Risach is willing to pay for artwork that has a "negative" value as long as the price paid equals the positive aesthetic value of the collection as a whole.

Mathilde also accumulates several works of art for her collection, among others her "masterpiece," the *Brunnennimphe*. This acquisition occurs after a relative of Mathilde's passes away. He had specifically requested that his collection be sold to a *Kunstliebhaber* only. It turns out that Mathilde can buy the piece for two reasons: first, because it will then stay in the family; and second, because it is expected that she will pay more for it than a non-relative would, thereby increasing the worth of the inheritance for the family: "Man gönnte es ihr mehr als einem Fremden, weil auf diese Weise das Kunstwerk gewissermaßen in der Familie blieb, und sie überdieß auch mehr in die gemeinschaftliche Erbschaft zahlte, als ein Fremder gethan haben würde" (2:230). This expectation that she will be willing to pay a higher price for the artwork seems peculiar, because one would expect that as an "insider" she would get a more favorable price than anyone else. The suggestion, of course, is that Mathilde, in her capacity as *Kunstliebhaber*, has a superior sense of the aesthetic value of the piece. This is translated into a willingness to equate this value with a fair monetary compensation. Furthermore, people outside of the inner circle of the *Asperhof* economy and its ideals would probably have attempted to arrive at a lower price and would thereby have operated according to the rules of the market economy. This then is an unmistakable judgment against the prevailing practices in that external economy.

The principle of paying a fair price can also be viewed as a fixation with fair representation. There has to be a concrete relationship between the substance (the aesthetic value of the artifact) and its expression of value (the monetary compensation for this artifact). Stifter resists the abstract representational practices of the modern economy in which supply and demand have taken on the demonic capacity to set prices that have no concrete grounding in the real value of products or the components that were used to create them.

The obsession with equating the aesthetic and monetary value of artifacts by paying a fair price, and thereby nullifying market forces, is yet another attempt to abandon the outside world of overconsumption, production, and market-driven exchange. The fair price principle makes the market economy disappear in the same way Stifter's autarchy does. In both cases an illusion is created; within the autarchy everything is economized (living off the interest, the "productive" use of time, and so forth); regarding the fair price, artifacts become reified as commodities. In other words, instead of the intended deeconomization of his narrative, Stifter accomplishes its total economization. The pattern of total economization emerges clearly in the exploration of Stifter's economopoetics. The common denominator is the illusory way in which his distancing from the economic results in a further integration of and reliance on economic patterns and structures.

Naming, Signification, and the Creation of Meaning

The characters of *Der Nachsommer* are always waiting for something, usually for the disclosure of some information that it is deemed too personal or too advanced given the young age of the recipient. Heinrich's father is waiting for Heinrich to discover that he knows Greek and Latin (2:161); Heinrich is waiting for von Risach to disclose his name throughout most of the story; von Risach is waiting for Heinrich to discover the beauty of the marble statue (2:75–6). Heinrich and Natalie, finally, are both filling their relationship with silence until the point when they reveal their love for each other, both awaiting that moment of connection (2:119; 259). Often, there seems to be a certain delay in conveying important information. In fact, the most significant aesthetic strategy employed in the novel is that of delayed naming. There are instances, when the generally accepted custom of introductions and naming is not of any great importance among the people connected with *Asperhof*. For example, while at a party at the nearby *Sternenhof*, Mathilde's estate, Heinrich ponders on the obvious absence of introductions: "Die Sitte des gegenseitigen Vorstellens der Personen, wie sie fast überall vorkömmt, scheint in dem Rosenhause und in dem Sternenhofe nicht strenge gebräuchlich zu sein[...] man überließ es eher dem Zufalle, mit einander bekannt zu werden[...]." which causes Heinrich to speculate: "Mich wollte man wahrscheinlich aus dem Spiele lassen, weil ich nie, wenn fremde Menschen in den Asperhof gekommen waren, gefragt hatte, wer sie seien" (2:210–11).

It is not only Heinrich's second family at the *Asperhof* and *Sternenhof* which participates in this avoidance of names; his father's house also condones this behavior. Interestingly, the whole family is in agreement with Heinrich's choice not to ask for von Risach's name: "Daß ich ihn nicht geradezu um seinen Namen gefragt habe, billigten alle meine Angehörigen, da er weit mehr gethan, nemlich mich aufgenommen und beherbergt habe, ohne um meinen Namen oder meine Herkunft zu forschen" (1:184). Eventually Heinrich sees von Risach in the city, but again has no opportunity to find out his name. Between Heinrich's first encounter with von Risach and the point when he finally finds out who his patron is, the narrative uses different names to refer to von Risach, such as *Aspermeier*, *Staatsmann* "Mann, der einmal in hohen Staatämtern gestanden war" (1:177; 179), and *Gastfreund*. Heinrich finally finds out a multitude of things about von Risach, but as he talks about him with his family everyone recommends that he leave things as they are and not probe for more information: "Man beschloß, in dieser Sache nicht weiter zu forschen, da mein Beherberger mir seinen Namen nicht freiwillig genannt habe, und die Dinge so zu belassen, wie sie seien" (1:206).

In what ways, then, is this avoidance of premature naming relevant to the aesthetic strategy of the novel, and how does this in turn relate to the economy? It is possible to connect this aesthetic strategy to a specific sentence in *Wien und die Wiener in Bildern aus dem Leben*, in which Stifter gives a rendition of the history of money from its innocuous beginnings as a mere facilitator of exchange to a state of all-pervasive corruption as an attractive means to satisfying an ever escalating frenzy of consumption. The passage in *Wien und die*

Wiener is a description of the *Münzhaus*, which initially is not named as such, but only referred to as "ein seltsam Haus."

> [...] man macht darinnen ein Ding, das an sich von geringem, man möchte sagen von gar keinem Gebrauche ist – aber durch Konvention schlummert in dem Ding der Inbegriff aller anderen, und es wird täglich erstrebt, heiß erstrebt von Millionen Händen, und täglich weggeworfen von Millionen Händen: das Geld, ein Ding, erst harmlos erdacht zur Bequemlichkeit der Menschen, ein holder, unbedeutender Vertreter der wahren Güter, um sie, die großen, plumpen, unbequemen, nicht allerorts mitführen zu dürfen – dann sachte wachsend in mählicher Bedeutung, unsäglichen Nutzen gewährend, Dinge und Völker vermischend in steigendem Verkehr, der feinste Nervengeist der Volksverbindungen – endlich ein Dämon, seine Farbe wechselnd, statt Bild der Dinge selbst Ding werdend, ja einzig Ding, das all die andern verschlang – ein blendend Gespenst, dem wir, als wäre es Glück, nachjagen, – ein rätselhafter Abgrund, aus dem alle Genüsse der Welt emportauchen, und in den wir dafür das höchste Gut dieser Erde hineingeworfen haben, die Bruderliebe... (GW, 35–6).[19]

As Peter Pfeiffer proposes, there is a structural similarity between the delayed naming of the *Münzhaus* and that of the main characters of *Der Nachsommer*. He states: "In that novel, too, there is a decisive resistance to premature naming for it would subject the named to the self-referential signifiers rather than reveal the full richness, individuality and particularity of meaning of the person and the object" (Pfeiffer, 82). His point is that this strategy of delayed naming in both works is a response to a semiotic crisis that arose with the development of a money economy as described in *Wien und die Wiener*. This semiotic crisis is due to the impossibility of proper signification because of the disappearance of a clear distinction between the "representation of things and the things themselves" (80). Pfeiffer interprets Stifter's usage of the money metaphor as a critique of the capitalist economy.[20] He also emphasizes how important these

19 I am citing from Stifter's *essay Wien und die Wiener* which appears under the title "Vom Sankt Stephansturme" in the 1959 edition of Stifter's *Gesammelte Werke*.

20 Also Martin and Erika Swales (1984) use this excerpt from *Wien und die Wiener* to shed light on Stifter's "painstaking litany of things and objects" as an attempt to resist the devaluations and abstractions of modern life (220). In their

economic metaphors and structures are to the aesthetics of Stifter's writing.

The strategy of delayed naming in turn gives rise to the excessive usage of the word "Ding" which does not involve any level of specificity. As a matter of fact, the word is the reincarnation of arbitrariness. As Pfeiffer puts it, "'Ding' becomes the signifier that is no longer 'Bild der Dinge' but, quite literally, 'Ding' itself and ingests all others" (85). The preferred status of the word "Ding" over specific names for things is a tactic that is intended to allow for full exploration of the object, person, or concept at hand. However, the outcome is the opposite: The more things that are included in the group that can be referred to as "Ding," the more severe the loss of connection to the real world. So in spite of Stifter's attempts to protect his text from the dangers of premature naming, the more self-referential his words become because, as Pfeiffer points out, "Ultimately, the word 'Ding' becomes the site where conventionality of signification and individuality of naming coincide" (85). It is precisely at this juncture that the word "Ding" coincides with money – both have an endless potential of expressing meaning, but at the same time this openness to signification leads to an inflation of sorts which destroys the potential for expressing individuality.

I have used Pfeiffer's notion of the paradoxical relationship between individuality and conventionality in my interpretation of Heinrich's development towards assimilation and conformity. The formation of my conceptual framework of total economization also builds on Pfeiffer's discussion of work, value, and time in *Der Nachsommer*.

There is one space in the *Rosenhaus* that is void of furniture and for a special purpose – the *Marmorsaal*. In a way, its function parallels that of the word *Ding*: It is nothing, but can be anything. Structurally, its representational capability resembles that of money. In her article "Equivocal Light of the Marmorsaal: Traces of Mysticism in Stifter's Novel, *Der Nachsommer*," Christine Sjögren

---

efforts to locate Stifter in relation to the charges of provincialism they employ a sociological approach that clarifies, for example, Stifter's position regarding modern society (219–21).

focuses her investigation on this unusual room. She outlines her reason for pursuing this study: "In this utopian novel, where functionalism is programmatic, a room empty and useless presents a baffling anomaly, which demands clarification" (Sjögren, 108).

Sjögren makes the point that the marble hall is different in nature from any other *Rosenhaus* space by refuting Heinrich's description of it as a collection of marble stones. She asserts instead that the entire room is made of marble and that the different marble pieces are not marked to designate them as parts of a collection. She points out that von Risach abstains from any comments about the room as he shows Heinrich around and in this way adds to the importance of his silence. This silence is diametrically opposed to his eloquent descriptions of the other rooms and their specific functions. Sjögren also draws attention to the fact that every visitor to the marble hall has to put on soft-soled slippers in order to protect the marble from unnecessary wear and tear. She interprets the shoe procedures as possibly religious in nature: "While the repeated mention of the shoe removal must indicate the noteworthy character of the hall, the act itself, observed in some religions as a ritual preliminary to entering a holy place, may here also have ritualistic connotation" (109).

While this religious aspect of the marble hall is interesting, even more intriguing are some of Sjögren's wordings as she continues to describe the space: "While the many things of *Nachsommer* express the author's ideology through their *Gestalt*, the marble hall is *gestaltlos*, is empty and silent. Its meaning cannot be deduced from qualities of form and material" (110). A similar hall at the *Sternenhof* is "likewise highly polished to mirror all things" (111). These descriptions could as well have been used to describe the function and nature of modern money. Money in itself is empty of value and meaning until it becomes defined by the political system within which it operates. In itself it does not carry any value – just like the marble hall, its meaning cannot be deduced from qualities of form and material. Once it has been assigned meaning, money has the ability to express and reflect all wishes. Stifter elevates the marble hall to the status of the general equivalent, the exclusive position of something to be the measure of all things. Money was raised into this same position of privilege and preferred representativeness. Money's position was cemented and turned into a monopoly of sorts. From having been just one commodity among others, it is now the measure of the value of all other commodities. Modern money in itself is empty: Its power lies in its ability to express and access other commodities of use value to individuals in society. In a way, it can be filled with anything. The marble hall similarly is empty but can be filled with anything – to reflect anything.

The signification process in *Der Nachsommer* relates to economics because structurally Stifter's strategy of delayed naming can be equated with a resistance against money's tendency towards inflationary representation and against the impending loss of individuality that is connected with its rise to power.

Work, Usefulness, and the Productive Use of Time

Stifter refers repeatedly to work in *Der Nachsommer* but as shown above, work does not refer to industrial production, nor is it limited to the purpose of capital accumulation. To the contrary, much of the work is concerned with activities in the realm of aesthetics. Though Stifter insists on the importance of work and adherence to a rigid time schedule, he is ambivalent about their meaning and content. The nature of his ambivalence is similar in structure to his strategy of delayed naming. He embraces these concepts while simultaneously expelling them from his narrative.

In von Risach's "work room" at the *Rosenhaus*, the activities taking place relate to artifacts, the estate, and to the planning of future projects: "Wenn man in dem Arbeitszimmer meines Gastfreundes versammelt war, besprach man gewöhnlich Angelegenheiten des Besizthums, Veränderungen, die nothwendig sind, Arbeiten, die man vornehmen müsse, und Gegenstände der Kunst" (Stifter, 1:224).

There are indications that work is an activity that is "invisible" – an activity of ease and purpose – almost to the extent that it undermines itself; i.e., that it is no longer work.[21] In von Risach's study, for example, there are no traces of work to be found. Everything is neatly put away in its proper place. Orderliness and utility appear to supersede the importance of the work itself. Ideal work should have the effortlessness of a performance by a virtuoso – it should just be, without leaving any byproduct: "Obwohl der alte Mann gesagt hatte, daß dieses Zimmer sein Arbeitszimmer sei, so waren doch keine unmittelbaren Spuren von Arbeit sichtbar. Alles schien in den Laden verschlossen oder auf seinen Platz gestellt zu sein" (1:90).

In addition, the borders between work and non-work, as well as those between usefulness and beauty, are blurred. The philosophy expressed in the text is that everything has its function and place. This is an aesthetics of the useful. Even the birds in the rose garden play an important role: "Die Vögel sind in diesem Garten unser Mittel gegen Raupen und schädliches Ungeziefer," (1:152) claims von Risach. They are not only there to provide beauty and music but to perform a function. Von Risach's "Vogelwirtschaft" has financial implications as well. He has performed a cost-benefit analysis of the situation as pertaining specifically to the fruit trees: "die Kosten aber sind in der That nicht ganz unbedeutend; allein wenn ich die edlen Früchte eines einzigen Pflaumenbaumes, welchen mir die Raupen der Vögel wegen

21 H. Rindisbacher (2002) adds an interesting perspective to the idea of invisible work. He defines Stifter's notion of work as being performed by those who are employed by privileged groups, individuals such as von Risach. Rindisbacher aptly points out that work, in the traditional sense of the word, i.e., the labors of those in pursuit of their daily bread, is not present in the novel: "It appears, instead, as the representative achievement of a social group, reified in its possessions and created not by this group but by others under its command" (200). Work is not necessarily focuses on the process of executing certain taskes, but in the result. The result of the work is preceeded by an "invisible action" executed by a laborer or craftsman (205). The restoration of old furniture and other objects, which is so prominent in *Der Nachsommer*, is a telling example of how this principle operates: "The real work is performed by those who do not participate in the novel's discourse. They and their work do not speak but are, instead, spoken to and spoken about. Work thus appears not as part of the plot of the novel, but 'only' as the central topic of its discourse" (205).

nicht abgefressen haben, verkaufe, so deckt der Kaufschilling die Nahrungskosten der Sänger ganz und gar. Freilich ist der Nuzen desto größer, je edler das Obst ist..." The work, claims von Risach, is not a hardship but rather a delight: "Die Mühe ist ein Vergnügen" (1:168). This passage points to the juxtaposition of the concept of work. The understanding of work and pleasure as being one concept differs acutely from the oppressive nature of early industrial employment. The aesthetics of the useful in *Der Nachsommer* is also part of the concept of total economization. Stifter is embedding his discussion of the economic in "harmless" topics such as the "bird economy" and thereby directing attention away from the economic thought that permeates *Der Nachsommer*.

Just as in Heinrich's father's house, each room at the *Rosenhaus* has a specific purpose. There are even certain parts of the house that do not have any specific function, but are only meant to be enjoyed visually; for example, those areas with such exquisite flooring that they warrant the usage of slippers: "die Abtheilungen, welche solche Fußböden haben, sind ja auch eigentlich nicht zum Bewohnen sondern nur zum Besehen bestimmt, und endlich gewinnt sogar das Besehen an Werth, wenn man es mit Beschwerlichkeit erkaufen muß" (1:94). It almost seems that the effort of changing shoes increases the aesthetic pleasure of the experience, that there is a synergy effect between the effort, or work, and the quality of the aesthetic experience.

Another discussion which again highlights the symbiosis between work and aesthetics takes place later in the text that. One evening, during dinner, von Risach and his circle discuss the planned restoration of the *Sternenhof* facade. They are concerned about the considerable cost involved in such a venture. Von Risach proposes that they should simply slow down the process so that the costs will be spread out over time. The interesting outcome of such a delay is to extend automatically the restoration process, and therefore the "work-pleasure" of creating the Beautiful: "da doch das Schaffen des Schönen das Vergnügen bilde, dieses Vergnügen sich verlängere" (2:224).

The connotation of "work" performed in the external economy is quite different from the "work-pleasure" that takes place at the *Rosenhaus*. First, the practicality and simple division of labor in the economic sense of the word are highlighted: “Gott lenkt es schon so, daß die Gaben gehörig vertheilt sind, so daß jede Arbeit gethan wird, die auf der Erde zu thun ist, und daß nicht eine Zeit eintritt, in der alle Menschen Baumeister sind.” The excerpt below expresses the notion that it is common for people to choose their occupation based on a measure of opportunism, or at least pragmatism:

> Es gibt solche, die sagen, sie seien zum Wohle der Menschheit Kaufleute Ärzte Staatsdiener geworden; aber in den meisten Fällen ist es nicht wahr. Wenn nicht der innere Beruf sie dahin gezogen hat, so verbergen sie durch ihre Aussage nur einen schlechteren Grund, nemlich daß sie den Stand als ein Mittel betrachteten, sich Geld und Gut und Lebensunterhalt zu erwerben (1:19).

This “other” work is best exemplified by Heinrich’s father’s career as a businessman. The nature of his work is described as monotonous and boring without the poetry evoked in *Soll und Haben*: “In Geschäfte der eintönigsten Art gezwungen, oder vielleicht selber und freiwillig in diese Geschäfte gegangen – denn er führte sie mit einer Ordnung mit einer Rechtlichkeit mit einer mit einer Anhänglichkeit an sie, daß man staunen mußte...” (2:160). In spite of the inferior nature of “business work,” the dedication of Heinrich’s father to his profession deserves a certain measure of respect, as the quote above reveals. When his father is studying a piece of art that Heinrich has brought him, Heinrich realizes the magnitude of the father’s sacrifice for him and his sister and is able to regard him with the utmost respect, and even awe, realizing that his father’s work is the basis of their whole existence:

> Mir klopfte das Herz vor Freude, und die weißen Haare, welche unter den dunkeln immer häufiger auf seinem Haupte zum Vorschein kamen, erschienen mir doppelt ehrwürdig, und die leichte Falte der Sorge auf seiner Stirne, die in der Arbeit für uns auf diesem Size seiner Gedanken entstanden war, während ich meiner Freude nachgehen und die Welt der Menschen genießen konnte, und während meine Schwester wie einen prachtvolle Rose erblühen durfte, erfüllte mich beinahe mit einer Andacht (2:15–16).

The beginnings of the father’s business were modest; he expanded his business, little by little until he eventually became “ein selbstständiger Kaufmann,” being able to do so with the assistance of his wife’s capital “eine nicht unbeträchtige Mitgift...” (2:177–8). There is much discussion about his retirement, even though it does not seem to happen as soon as his family wishes. There is always some business activity interfering with his retirement and freedom to travel: “die Geschäfte seien immer dringend, und sein Mißtrauen in die Kräfte der jüngeren Leute wachse immer mehr, je älter er werde, und je mehr er selber alle Sachen allein verrichten wolle” (1:185). When the family discusses a visit to the *Rosenhaus*, the father affirms the importance of his business, stating that he cannot commit to a trip because of his obligations to the business and his dependence on it: “binden, wißt ihr, kann sich ein Mann nicht, der von seinem Geschäft abhängt, und nicht wissen kann, welche Umstände einzutreten vermögen, die von ihm Zeit und Handlungen fordern” (2:50).

A comparison between Drendorf and von Risach exposes their very different attitudes toward professional activities. Drendorf clearly has accepted his financial dependence on his business and is therefore willing to make the necessary sacrifices on a personal and familial level. Von Risach, on the other hand, never quite reconciled with his duties as a public servant. As Wolfgang Albrecht points out in his article, “Geschäft, Genuss, Gemeinnutz: Korrelationen und Traditionen der ästhetisierten Lebens-Ordnung in Stifters *Nachsommer*,” there is a frequent usage of the term *Geschäft* in the first chapter of *Der Nachsommer*. The professional activities in the realm of business are the foundation of all *Kunsterwerb*. Albrecht compares Drendorf’s and von Risach’s relationships to their respective professional careers. Von Risach experiences the conflict and withdraws because he cannot fulfill his business responsibilities with pleasure and gives up his primary profession as a government employee in order to devote all his time to aesthetic projects.

Drendorf on the other hand is able to coexist between the two opposing demands according to the principle – first business, then pleasure! Heinrich’s father manages to pursue a career as a businessman while devoting any spare time to his artistic and literary interests: “Berufsobliegenheiten gehen ihm zeitlebens vor; der Kunst und Literatur widmet er sich nach getaner Arbeit oder dann, wenn er sich ‘einen Augenblick abkargen’ kann [...]. Der Kaufmann Drendorf vermag Metier und Liebhaberei in erfüllter Lebensführung zu bringen" (Albrecht, 1–2).

Albrecht draws attention to the fact that one of the main principles of business and trade, independence, has a great influence on Heinrich's education; already early on he distances himself from employing a new tutor, because he wants to learn on his own. Heinrich is also given access to his capital prior to his actual becoming of age, which allows him an increased measure of freedom. In spite of their different viewpoints, both father figures are equally manifest in their position as authoritative role model to Heinrich because of their exemplary business and general behavior: "Die Autorität des Familienoberhaupts, die auch Risach besitzt, steht außer jeglichem Zweifel, zumal sie in beiden Fällen exemplarisch auf kompetentes Tun statt auf konventionelle Machtansprüche gegründet ist" (6).

It is typical of the modern economy that it quantifies work and that it is driven by time constraints. In the modern industrial economy, there is also a dichotomy between time spent at work and at leisure. Even though the *Nachsommer* economy distances itself from the modern economy, it still deals with time in similar ways. Here again, we have an example of how *Der Nachsommer* adheres to the principles of the modern economy while simultaneously expelling them from its narrative. Peter Pfeiffer discusses the relevance of time to the *Nachsommer* characters. He draws a parallel between Heinrich's position outside the "modern consumption-based economy" and his adherence to time schedules and "productive time." In spite of this position, Heinrich profits from the capitalist economy by earning interest on his inheritance. While his life is ruled by strict schedules and the principles of capitalist time pressures, he still does not produce anything. He is both a participant and a non-participant at the same time. As Pfeiffer puts it: "[...] the effective, 'full' use of time is empty in terms of a capitalist production or profit orientation and contradicts directly Marx's analysis of capitalist utilization. For Stifter, effective use of time becomes an end in itself, a ritualized avoidance of idle time." Pfeiffer interprets this time orientation as a way of avoiding meaningless consumption (Pfeiffer, 83).

Early on as Heinrich pursues studies in mathematics, he economizes his time in order to optimize his learning: "Ich sezte mir bestimmte Zeiträume fest, in welchen ich vom Weitergehen abließ, um das bis dahin Errungene wiederholen, und meinem Gedächtnisse einprägen zu können, ehe ich zu ferneren Theilen vorwärtsschritt" (Stifter, 1:27). This relationship to time is reinforced by Heinrich's encounter with von Risach. Making good use of his time is something he has adopted from the *Rosenhaus*: "Da dort der Werth der Zeit sehr hoch angeschlagen, und dieses Gut sehr sorgfältig angewendet wurde, so fing ich, wenn ich mir auch bisher einen großen Vorwurf nicht hatte machen können, dennoch an, mit viel mehr Ordnung als bisher nach einem einzigen Ziele während einer bestimmten Zeit hinzu-arbeiten..." (1:230).

Obviously, time is viewed as a commodity in the *Rosenhaus* economy. Time is a monetarized asset of which the possessor has ownership, one which cannot be squandered. When von Risach invites Heinrich to come back to the *Rosenhaus* to spend some relaxing, unstructured time there he tells him: "lebt einmal eine Weile müßig bei uns, das heißt, thut, was Euch der Augenblick und die Neigung eingibt" (2:45). There is unmistakably a separation of work and leisure time in the novel, just as as one would expect in an industrial economy. Von Risach's recommendation that Heinrich live without a strict schedule for a while is an exception to the reigning rules concerning productive time in the Stifter's text. The specific context here relates to Heinrich's educational pursuit. Von Risach believes that Heinrich needs a break because he started his specialization too early in life. Heinrich, having been conditioned by his father's example, has a difficult time accepting life without a structured plan and time constraints. He resumes his professional activities in the field of sciences and thereby returns to the time constraints associated with the industrial market economy: "Meinen Beruf, den ich im Sommer beiseite gesetzt hatte, nahm ich wieder auf. Ich machte mir gleichsam Vorwürfe, daß ich ihn so verlassen und mich einem planlosen Leben hatte hingeben können" (2:171).

In addition to the reading of the productive use of time as a safeguard against consumption, as Pfeiffer does, the employment of this capitalist principle can also be interpreted as a way of equating the importance of aesthetic production with that of industrial production. By implementing similar time pressures and principles of economizing with time, Stifter casts aesthetic production as similar in structure to industrial production. Within Stifter's symbiotic system of work and pleasure, a facet of criticism is added to the formula because of the positive nature of the work-pleasures at the *Rosenhaus* compared to the negative depiction of the "external" work in the modern economy.

The Economy of Realism

The preferred form of artistic expression in *Der Nachsommer* is debatable. The quality and craftsmanship of all the work that is being done with artifacts is superior, both in the realm of practical restoration and replication work and in the planning, categorization, and organizational phases. However, the text often argues that Heinrich is not a great artist. The purpose of his drawings is to complement the descriptions of the objects of natural science that he investigates. His dabbling with artistic expression as he paints landscapes can be categorized as mediocre at best. Heinrich himself is the first to admit this fact:

> Obgleich meine Malereien keine Kunstwerke waren, wie ich jetzt immer mehr einsah, so hatten sie doch einen Vorzug, den ich erst später recht erkannte, und der darin bestand, daß ich nicht wie ein Künstler nach Abrundung nach zusammenstimmender Wirkung oder Anwendung von Schulregeln rang, sondern mich ohne vorgefaßter Einübung den Dingen hingab, und sie so darzustellen suchte, wie ich sie sah. Dadurch gewannen sie, was sie auch an Schmelz und Einheit verloren, an Naturwahrheit in einzelnen Stücken, und gaben dem Nichtkenner und dem, der nie die Gebirge gesehen hatte, eine bessere Vorstellung als schöne und künstlerisch vollendete Gemälde, wenn sie nicht die vollendetsten waren, die dann freilich auch die Wahrheit im höchsten Maße trugen (2:53).

Any deficiency in aesthetic expression is compensated by the capacity of his paintings to capture reality accurately. The purpose of his paintings is to serve as a medium for those people who have not seen a certain object or spectacular view. Through Heinrich's paintings, they can gain access to the original beauty of the painted object. This is exactly what happens with Heinrich's sister, Klotilde, who claims that she now knows what the mountains look like even though she has never been there (2:53).

In one of his early visits to the *Rosenhaus*, Heinrich views some of the drawings in von Risach's possession. The drawings show different buildings in their entirety, as well as their separate parts. Heinrich wonders wherein lies the quality of these drawings made by Eustach, a young artist who works and lives with von Risach, and concludes that, in part, it has something to do with the coloring technique. There is a certain measure of economization in the usage of colors: "Immer aber waren die Farben so untergeordnet gehalten, daß die Zeichnungen nicht in Gemälde übergingen, sondern Zeichnungen blieben, die durch die Farbe nur noch mehr gehoben wurden." Therefore they will not distract the eye of the viewer from the substance of the drawing: "daß die Dinge als Dinge nicht als Färbungen gelten" (1:103). Another peculiar aspect of these drawings is that, in spite of Eustach's superior technique, they are not perfect. Interestingly, this is not attributed to a flaw in the artist but rather to the fact that the original is imperfect. If the original is somewhat faulty, evidently the drawing has to reflect that truthfully. In Heinrich's eyes, these flaws only enhance the representational quality of the drawings: "Es gewannen durch diesen Umstand die Zeichnungen in meinen Augen noch mehr, da er gerade ihre große Treue bewies" (1:104).

As Heinrich further pursues his painting, he asks von Risach and Eustach for their opinion: "Ihr Urtheil ging einstimmig darauf hinaus, daß mir das Naturwissenschaftliche viel besser gelungen sei als das Künstlerische" (2:36). As they talk about the characteristics of good art, two issues come to the fore of the discussion. First, vision is an important component in artistic production, but only in its support of the soul that is the real originator of art: "Das Auge soll nur geübt und unterrichtet werden, die Seele müsse schaffen, das Auge soll ihr dienen." Second, Eustach points out the impossibility of "perfect" mimesis, specifically when it comes to landscapes. Capturing the scene's full "identity" is not possible. To reckon with this problem, Eustach claims that the solution is to compromise the level of detail: "lieber unbestimmter als bestimmter zu sein." In his view art and effect are most important: "Wenn überhaupt ein Fehler gegen die Genauigkeit gemacht werden müsse – und kein Mensch könne Dinge, namentlich Landschaften, in ihrer völligen Wesenheit geben –, so sei es besser, die Gegenstände großartiger und übersichtlicher zu geben, als in zu viele einzelne Merkmale zerstreut. Das erste sei das Künstlerischere und Wirksamere" (2:37). As Eustach sees it, the complete coverage of all the small details is not what defines the piece of art. Instead, completeness in artistic expression as a whole is the qualifying factor of the aesthetic value of a piece of art.

The marble statue is a perfect example of how *Der Nachsommer* endorses a concept of holistic beauty that is reminiscent of antique aesthetic ideals. There is no one specific characteristic that makes the Greek marble statue beautiful. Von Risach says: "Das ist eben das Wesen der besten Werke der alten Kunst, und ich glaube, das ist das Wesen der höchsten Kunst überhaupt, daß man keine einzelnen Theile oder einzelne Absichten findet, von denen man sagen kann, das ist das schönste, sondern das Ganze ist schön, von dem Ganzen möchte man sagen, es ist das schönste; die Theile sind blos natürlich" (2:87).

In a discussion about issues of realist representation, it is useful to project implications in the realm of the plastic arts to that of literature. In *Reflections of Realism: Paradox, Norm and Ideology in Nineteenth-Century German Prose*, Robert Holub demonstrates how the recognition of beauty in the plastic arts occurs simultaneously with allusion to a literary art form. There is a long series of such associations throughout the novel; Holub writes: "Both von Risach and Heinrich's father have a passion for paintings and books, and each is accorded equal respect in their collections. When Heinrich begins his scientific expeditions, he uses two methods to record his observations: written reports and sketches." The easy transition from painting/ sculpture to poetry/literature in *Der Nachsommer*, Holub claims, is characteristic of realism (Holub, 68–9). Stifter's account of Heinrich's efforts in drawing and painting leads me to conclude that he gives definite preference to pictorial replications over literary renditions. Russell Berman likewise focuses on this point in *The Rise of the*

Modern German Novel: Crisis and Charisma, "not only does he insist that the picture reproduces the object with greater success than does verbal discourse, but he treats the pictorial image as in fact superior to the unmediated observation of the observed object itself" (Berman, 123).

It takes Heinrich some time to come to a true realization of Beauty. He has seen the marble statue many times before when it all falls into place for him, but never quite understood the extent of its beauty, until he suddenly experiences an aha-moment that initiates a change in his perspective: "Ich blickte auf die Bildsäule, und sie kam mir heute ganz anders vor" (Stifter, 2:73). When Heinrich approaches von Risach about this revelation and asks him why he never told him about the beauty of the marble statue, von Risach replies: "Jemanden sagen, daß etwas schön sei [...] heißt nicht immer, jemanden den Besiz der Schönheit geben." To answer Heinrich's question what he had thought of him because of his failure to recognize the statues's beauty, von Risach explains: "Ich habe gedacht, daß ihr wahrhaftig seid [...] und ich habe euch höher geachtet als die, welche ohne Überzeugung von dem Werke reden, oder als die, welche es darum loben, weil sie hören, daß es von andern gelobt wird" (2:76). Von Risach admires and respects Heinrich's progression towards this realization. In his eyes, it sets Heinrich apart from those who talk about the statue from a superficial perspective, those who have not reached Heinrich's understanding of Beauty.

It is at this exact point that von Risach feels that he should divulge how the statue came into in his possession. Some time ago, when in Italy, he found it stored in a hall among some other pieces of sculpture. Even though the statue was covered in plaster, von Risach was able to see through it to the nucleus of its beauty. The Italian owner, however, did not. The son of the owner wanted to get rid of a number of the pieces in order to create a new space where all the art would be of the same size and motif. He had already ordered a set of new plaster pieces to that end:

> Ihr Sohn, der sich durch Handel Geld erworben, werde den Plaz in einen Saal mit Säulen verwandeln, es werden Tische herum stehen, und es werden vornehme Fremde kommen, sich hier zu ergözen. Die Gestalten müssen weg,

> weil sie ungleich seien, und weil Menschen und Thiere unter einander stehen, ihr Sohn habe schon die schönsten Gipsarbeiten bestellt, die alle gleich groß wären (2:77).

There are a few implications that emerge from von Risach's account. First, money is of no benefit unless the owner has aesthetic insight. The fact that the son has acquired riches through his business does not enable him to make aesthetically solid choices as he purchases his art. To the contrary, the connotation is the opposite. The "contextlessness" of being *noveau riche* seems to preclude any sound aesthetic decision on his part. Second, the creation of a unified impression, as was the intention with the purchase of the new pieces, is not a guarantee of beauty. In this case, the *intention* of the unified impression spoils everything. The display becomes an affected and tacky juxtaposition of plaster statues that are not even the "real thing" – in this case marble. In aesthetic terms, the word that comes to mind is *Schwulst*, a word that Stifter had used in a different context as I show below. In economic terms this would be rendered as "inflated representation." The plaster statues cannot possess "complete" aesthetic value because there is no correspondence between the aesthetic expression of a respective statue and the value of its substance as is the case for a genuine marble statue. In the money economy this is the state of a deceptive government printing and minting money beyond its economy's production capacity, a situation that will eventually create excessive inflation. The same is true for the field of aesthetics if solid quality art is being undermined by the proliferation of deceptive copies.

During his exploration of literature, Heinrich reads some authors who seek to evoke the same kind of effect by misrepresenting reality:

> Unter den Büchern waren auch solche, in denen Schwulst enthalten war. Sie gaben die Natur in und außer dem Menschen nicht so, wie sie ist, sondern sie suchten sie schöner zu machen, und suchten besondere Wirkungen hervorzubringen. Ich wendete mich von ihnen ab. Wem das nicht heilig ist, was ist, wie wird der besseres erschaffen können, als was Gott erschaffen hat? In der Naturwissenschaft war ich gewohnt geworden, auf die Merkmale der Dinge zu achten, diese Merkmale zu lieben, und die Wesenheit der Dinge zu verehren. Bei den Dichtern des Schwulstes fand ich gar keine Merkmale, und es erschien mir endlich lächerlich, wenn einer schaffen wollte, der nichts gelernt hat (2:33).

Here again it is evident that Heinrich's background in the sciences plays an important role in developing his potential for and appreciation of artistic understanding and expression. A later discussion between Heinrich and von Risach contemplates a preferential position of literature. Von Risach sets forth: "nur die Dichtkunst hat beinahe gar keinen Stoff mehr, ihr Stoff ist der Gedanke in seiner weitesten Bedeutung, das Wort ist nicht der Stoff, es ist nur der Träger des Gedankens, wie etwa die Luft den Klang an unser Ohr führt. Die Dichtkunst ist daher die reinste und höchste unter den Künsten" (2:39). In fact, von Risach reveres literature to such a degree that he collects books in languages that he cannot read, because they are testimonies to the greatness of literature.

Von Risach's notion that the word is not the substance of literature but merely the transmitter of thought is problematic. He compares the word to the air that transmits sound. Because of this imagined neutrality and transparency between the word and the thought to which it refers, von Risach considers literature to be the highest art form. This somewhat simplistic idea does not take into consideration the inevitably subjective input and interpretive capability of the originator of any literary text. Von Risach's view is parallel to an economy using gold coins whose representational powers are concrete and non-symbolic. It is a world where things are what they say they are. Conversely, the principles of a paper money economy do not correspond to these ideals. A paper money economy uses more mediated modes of representation and allows for abstraction and symbolism.

In his article "Prescribing Reality: The Preface as a Device of Literary Realism in Auerbach, Keller and Stifter," Hans P. Gabriel discusses how these three authors use prefaces to frame their novella collections as realistic stories. According to Gabriel, the authors differ in their prefatory approaches but are united in their conscious attempts at objectivity. He adds: "Taken together, these prefaces corroborate the modern critical emphasis on necessary authorial interference in literary realism" (Gabriel, 326). As Gabriel rightfully observes, Stifter insists on the real world connections of his novellas, all the while still conscious of the constructed nature of his texts.

This line of thought about Stifter's brand of realism has parallels within the *Nachsommer* narrative because when von Risach elevates poetry to the highest of all art forms he, in essence, marginalizes the aspect of mediation. Furthermore, there are numerous discussions about pictorial art and strategies for accomplishing the most accurate depiction of reality. In addition, the fashion in which Risach "domesticates" nature around the *Rosenhaus* and how his constructed "naturalness" is preferred to the original, untouched nature, shows that his arguments about poetry are not that uncomplicated, especially within the context of the aesthetic thought of the novel. There is a clear paradox between reality and artifice.

Helena Ragg-Kirby also uses Stifter's "Vorrede" to *Bunte Steine* as a departure point for her exploration of the author's narrative objectivity. In her article "'Eine immerwährende Umwandlung der Ansichten': Narrators and Their Perspectives in the Works of Adalbert Stifter," she argues that Stifter's works offer no narrative objectivity: "Stifter's world is entirely 'gedeutet': interpreted by the narrators, the readers, the characters. His work insidiously questions and deconstructs, not through direct questioning but by the way in which the narrative perspective constantly shifts, by the way in which all he overtly vaunts, he covertly undermines" (Ragg-Kirby, 142–3). According to Ragg-Kirby, Stifter's technique is that of "telling less by telling more." She uses comparisons between Stifter's *Journal* and *Buchfassungen* to illustrate her point. It would be expected that the much longer book editions would offer proportionally more information, but as Ragg-Kirby points out, much of the textual space is devoted to details that divert attention from the real issues at hand, and sometimes the additional information opens up more gaps than it fills: "In fact, however, much of the 'information' reveals itself to be digressive, not to say diversionary" (130).

This strategy of "telling less by telling more" is typical of Stifter's narratives. Related to this strategy is his trend to give information in the negative. According to Ragg-Kirby "This is a masterly style whereby the reader is given finely wrought information, but information that is so to speak a minus quantity." She exemplifies how in *Der Nachsommer*, Stifter tends to focus much attention on what people are not saying and the fact that they are not present. In other words, textual references to silence and absence fill the text with information that is not particularly helpful. Ragg-Kirby contends that "Stifter thus shifts to a narrative that is blatantly reticent, elliptical, and suppressive about essentials, while concomitantly tending to lay a smokescreen of inessential detail" (130). In my discussion of Stifter's strategy of delayed naming it was precisely this sense of silence between characters, the absence of essential information, and the reluctance to ascribe a final definition to people by not using their names, that came to the fore. My interpretation of this phenomenon focused on the paradoxical dynamics between the endless possibility of signification and the loss of specificity in *Der Nachsommer*. Ragg-Kirby's observations concerning Stifter's lack of objectivity can be interpreted in a similar fashion: All the while Stifter imbues his narrative with obsessive descriptiveness and amazing attention to detail, he yet fails his own realistic approach by allowing his characters and narrators to contradict not only each other but also the reader.[22]

In his essay "Adalbert Stifter and the Scope of Realism" Eric Downing focuses on the function of the telescope in Stifter's prose and its relation to his realism. Downing writes that the telescope affirms the idea of "vision as not about the simple objective recording of an empirical reality, but instead about the complex – and not only psychological – imposition of a meaning, law, and order behind that reality." He continues "For all Stifter's protagonists, telescopes become their means of mastering the world, for establishing that initially unperceived, and so also in a sense absent, order that transforms the view into something 'real' for them" (Downing, 2–3). Downing investigates the extent of telescopic vision as a neutral, scientific medium or "artificial, mechanized" eyes, and finds that the "telescopes render ambivalent whether the law and order they assist in determining is a quality of the perceiver or the scene." According to Downing, this kind of ambivalence is characteristic of poetic realism.

22 Eva Geulen (1998) has written an article entitled "Depicting Description: Lukács and Stifter" in which she points out that Stifter's desire to legitimize what is seen and said in a description tends to undermine systematically the paradigms that appear to govern the description (2).

He points out that the association of telescopes with stasis, and stasis with realism, is particularly insistent in Stifter's *Der Hochwald*: "The reproduction of the same representation, and the repeated reproduction of the same representation throughout the narrative, even in the language used, serves to negate a sense of narrative progress or change, to insist on the represented reality as still, and its stillness and reproducibility as the guarantee of its reality" (5).

This narrative strategy is prevalent also in *Der Nachsommer*. A couple of patterns emerge: First, the order and constancy of the rooms is a way of fixing reality, to force it to stay intact in order to allow for – and guarantee – realist representation. Second, the whole procedure involved in Heinrich's repeated returns to the *Rosenhaus* does not evolve over time. Each and every time he inspects the premises with von Risach; they look at the different buildings and the activities taking place there. Above all though, they always revisit the blossoming roses. As Sabine Schmidt phrases it: "Den Höhepunkt bildet dabei die zum 'religiösen' Zeremoniell, zum Ritus gewordene gemeinsame Betrachtung der blühenden Rosen" (Schmidt, 88). This sense of cyclical repetition, Schmidt interprets as a structurally similar to the mythical narrative.

In my view, Downing's idea of "telescopic" stasis is more informative for the exploration of Stifter's realism. The many instances in which Stifter is torn between objectivity and subjectivity, as well as the openness in signification and individuality, the insistence on cyclical patterns and static sceneries, represent an attempt to reinforce his realism.

Another concept that relates to Stifter's realism is the process of imitation, which is integrated into the novel on different levels. This process is partly based on a clear sense of agreement among the protagonists. Very seldom is there any dissidence. This holds true not only for the types of dissidence "typical" of the educational novel, such as generational friction and conflicting interests between individual and society, but the lack of imitation is also part of the programmatic make-up of the novel. I again cite Robert Holub who draws attention to the fact that imitation is all-pervasive in *Der Nachsommer*; "almost every character in the novel is involved with some sort of mimetic activity." As previously mentioned, there is no real conflict between scientist and artist because because both have the same task: copying and preserving reality. Imitation is thus a natural, universal activity not necessarily restricted to the realm of aesthetics. There is no pronounced discrepancy between scientist and artist because the scientist is not thought to be an "inventor or experimenter but as the humble discoverer of an already given reality" (Holub, 72). To a certain extent then, science is a mimetic activity just like art. That being said, it becomes necessary to identify exactly what kind of mimetic structures prevail in *Der Nachsommer*.

As indicated above, the lack of conflict manifests the ideal of conformity and the adoption of certain prescribed values and ideas. Heinrich effortlessly appropriates these values by observing von Risach. Thus an act of imitation takes place because Heinrich emulates his role model. At the same time, learning about imitation is certainly the main objective in Heinrich's education. Holub believes that Heinrich's account, the text of *Der Nachsommer*, is more than a simple imitation of reality: "It is an imitation of an imitation, and as such partakes of a complex mimetic nature in which theme (mimesis in art, imitation in education), style (description as the dominant mode of presentation), and composition (autobiography as imitation of one's own life) reinforce one another" (77).

In conclusion then, I will argue that Heinrich's learning process within the realm of aesthetics is concerned primarily with the ability to imitate reality "correctly," to find an expression of realism. It also involves the ability to read signs: when Heinrich first enters the sphere of the *Rosenhaus*, his decision originates in his inability to read the signs of nature; in this case to predict the weather. It is paramount that this episode presents the only difference in opinion between Heinrich and von Risach. During the remainder of the novel, every dialogue is marked by reciprocal agreement between the involved parties. This avoidance of conflict, in all its different shapes and forms, is indicative of a preoccupation with balance and harmony.

The harmonizing attitude toward education is only one aspect of this tendency.

For Heinrich the educational process involves his scientific pursuits and their subsequent incorporation into his endeavors in the field of aesthetic expression. Ultimately, he arrives at a stage of aesthetic realization that involves his understanding of the Beautiful. He learns the virtue of avoiding *Schwulst* and of appreciating Classic ideals of simplicity and of a seemingly transparent mediation as exemplified in Risach's notion of *Dichtkunst*. The process itself is based on the imitation of the father figures and the adoption of certain values in the realm of both economies, the aesthetic and the material.

Inheritance and the Sublimation of the Fathers

As on the final pages of *Soll und Haben*, there is an act of opening accounting books in *Der Nachsommer*. When Heinrich's union with Natalie becomes public, his father informs Heinrich about his business and all its financial aspects: "Er erzählte mir endlich von seinem kaufmännischen Geschäfte, und machte mich mit dessen Grundlagen und Stellungen bekannt" (Stifter, 3:79). Analogously to *Soll und Haben*, there is a sense of starting anew, of one generation giving way to the next. In discussions with his wife concerning his retirement, Heinrich's father informs his wife: "Ich werde doch einmal, meine liebe Therese mein Buch abschließen[...] und es wird für mich der Stillstand der Geschäfte eintreten. Sie mögen in andere Hände übergehen, oder sich ganz auflösen" (3:42). The revelation and the giving over of the books is only one way of passing on the torch from one generation to the next. The other way is through inheritance.

The idea of inheritance is equally important to the two fathers in the novel, Drendorf, Heinrich's natural father, and von Risach, Heinrich's foster father so to speak. In both cases their wives contributed considerable dowries; other money in the form of inheritances also comes into play in their lives. Stifter portrays both fathers as competent men who followed their own professional paths regardless of these monetary contributions. Throughout the novel, Heinrich's father Drendorf is a hard and diligent worker who is dedicated to his business. Similarly, von Risach, when describing his marriage in a conversation to Heinrich, points out that he himself had accumulated considerable assets before the union with his wife:

> Meine Gattin hatte mir eine namhafte Mitgift gebracht, aber ich hätte eine größere Gabe hinzulegen können. Da ich in meinem mäßigen Leben beinahe nichts brauchte, so hatte ich, besonders da ich einmal in höherer Stellung war, bedeutende Ersparungen gemacht. Diese legte ich in den damaligen Staatspapieren nieder, und da dieselben nach Beendigung des Krieges ansehnlich stiegen, so war ich beinahe ein reicher Mann (3:215–16).

Von Risach's wife dies after only twyears and, after another year, a considerable inheritance comes his way: "Ein Jahr nach dem Tode Juliens starb mein Oheim, und sezte mich zu dem Erben seines beträchtlichen Vermögens ein" (3:216).

Towards the end of the book the familial arrangements between the three families are discussed in great detail. The narrative focuses much attention on financial aspects, specifically on those having to do with inheritance. Von Risach explains to Heinrich: "Natalie erhält von mir den Asperhof mit allem, was in ihm ist, nebst meinen Barschaften[...]. Die Schriften bezüglich der Übertragung meines Vermögens an Natalien werden ihr nach der Vermählung eingehändigt werden. So lange ich lebe, erhält sie einen Theil, den Rest nach meinem Tode[...]. Natalie erhält auch nach ihrer Vermählung den Theil, der ihr aus dem Nachlasse ihres Vaters Tarona gebührt" (3:225–6). The above conversation is quite personal, and its content has important financial implications for the future of the young couple. It is noteworthy that at the moment when von Risach divulges the name of Natalie's father, Tarona, Heinrich is completely surprised: "Ist Nataliens Name Tarona?" (3:226). He had not known the last name of his fiancée up until that moment. In accordance with the principle of delayed naming, it could be argued that Natalie is explored to her fullest potential, even in terms of establishing her net worth, before she finally is "crowned" with the name Tarona.

In his essay "The Place of Inheritance in the Bildungsroman," M.R. Minden discusses the relationship between the motif of inheritance, the concept of art, and the notion of *Bildung*. Minden points out: "Both Drendorf and von Risach display an almost voluptuous love for testamentary detail" (Minden, 35). In addition, drawing from the poetic quality of the novel's testamentary passages, Minden interprets these statements as utmost expressions of love. These passages offer an "accumulated feeling that love has no stronger form of expression than that conveyed in the words: 'you shall inherit everything I own'" (36). The fact that Stifter has created two fathers from whom Heinrich inherits is of relevance to Minden as a sign of the "circularity of inheritance," a circularity that counterbalances the linearity of progression that is a common trait of the *Bildungsroman* (34). There are clear parallels between the two father figures – Minden goes so far as to use the term "identity." Heinrich's educational journey and personal development are not so much progressive paths towards the ideal of the father, but rather circular movements between two poles. Minden explains: "the very function of the ride from image to image, from Drendorf to Risach, is to insist upon the identity of these two terminal points, and not to describe any sort of progress" (37). Minden's theory corroborates my earlier claim that Heinrich's personality does not really crystallize, but that he becomes a replica of the Father, that his individuality is sacrificed to conventionality. Not only does he become like the fathers, but he also acquires features that are characteristic of money. Money likewise has no individuality and does not discriminate between the different purposes for which it is being used. In addition, conventionality is the basis for its success as a facilitator of exchange. In a money economy objects and people lose individuality and money becomes the defining denominator of value.

Minden considers the relevance of art in *Der Nachsommer*. The sense of identity with which Minden characterizes the two father figures becomes especially evident in their appreciation and ownership of art. As Minden points out, "Art is both the expression or even shrine of spiritual values *and* something which can be possessed and thus passed on" (38). Within the realm of Stifter's economy, the transmission of property through inheritance takes place by means of legal documentation, a process which perpetuates the social order within which the protagonist exists. The symbolism of the inherited art collections is of notability to Minden: "Stifter is linking the non-material values implicit in the collections with the social stability guaranteed by the laws of the inheritance or transfer of property" (38). This symbolic power of the inheritance is the deciding factor, not the purchasing power of the assets *per se*. This is certainly a notable and interesting aspect, but it is not the only one. Inheritance is also relevant in the arena of paternal competition that develops towards the end of the novel. The friendly, yet still significant, competition between the fathers results in what can be described as their neutralization. Every part of the "competition" ends in a tie. All equations end in parity, and the fathers emerge equally strong from their encounters in the realms of aesthetics and economics.

Because of his socioeconomic position, there is a sense that von Risach is superior to Drendorf throughout most of the novel. However, after they meet and get acquainted, there are indications that Heinrich's father has unexpected monetary and aesthetic assets. For example, when von Risach visits Heinrich's family in town, he alludes to the fact that Drendorf's art collection is more valuable than his own: "In Hinsicht der Bilder meines Vaters sprach sich mein Gastfreund dahin aus, daß sie als ganzes durchaus werthvoller seien als seine Sammlung…" (Stifter, 3:253).

In addition, at the wedding ceremony two beautiful necklaces are given to Natalie by the fathers, one of emeralds and one of diamonds and rubies.[23] Von Risach's diamond and ruby necklace is said to complement Natalie's beauty. The emeralds from Heinrich's father are described in more general terms; basically as being very beautiful in spite of being relatively small. However, what warrants the greatest attention is again the setting: "Nicht nur waren die Steine an sich, obwohl nicht zu den größten ihrer Art gehörend, sehr schön, sondern die Fassung, die Steine nicht drückend, war doch so leicht und so schön, daß das Ganze wie ein zusammengehöriges in einander gewachsenes Werk wie ein wirkliches Kunstwerk erschien" (3:267). The competition between the two has no winner, because each necklace carries a different aesthetic function: "War der Diamantschmuck wie fromm erschienen, so erschien der Smaragdschmuck wie heldenartig. Keiner erhielt den Preis. Risach und der Vater stimmten selber überein" (3:269).

23 In her article "Adalbert Stifters Nachsommer: Subjektive Idealität: Heinrich Drendorfs Subjektkonstitution im Spiegel seiner Selbstdefinition," Sabine Schmidt uses the scene in which Natalie shows the wedding party the two necklaces to demonstrate how she is reduced to a piece of art – an Ausstellungsbüste (98–9).

Von Risach himself employs vocabulary belonging to the concept of competition when he addresses Heinrich's father: "Da heute unser Wettkampf unentschieden geblieben ist, [...] so wollen wir nun sehen, wer mit geringerem Aufwande seinen Siz zu einem größeren Kunstwerke machen kann, du deinen Drenhof, oder wenn du ihn lieber Gusterhof nennen willst, oder ich meinen Asperhof." Eustach, in support of von Risach, declares himself willing to share the workforce with Drendorf: "Wenn es uns im Asperhofe an Arbeit fehlt, so werden wir in den Drenhof hinübergeliehen." Von Risach, who now calls Drendorf his enemy, extends this offer even further: "Auch dann, wenn wir hier Arbeit haben, [...] ich will dem Feinde Waffen liefern" (3:270). While it is true that this is all said in jest, and that the nature of the competition is friendly, the terminology of competition still carries meaning because it is the defining topic of discussion on the wedding day. This whole discourse is initiated by the ceremonial procedures surrounding the legal documents.

After the church service there is much discussion of how these legal papers outline the financial situation of the new couple: "Da wir wieder in dem Marmorsaale waren, wurden auf den langen Tisch, den man heute hier aufgerichtet und mit vielen Stühlen umgeben hatte, von Risach und von meinem Vater die Papiere niedergelegt, die sich auf unsere Vermählung und unser Vermögen bezogen" (3:261). A special table has been set up for the display of these documents in the marble hall – the space connected with money and its ability to signify anything and everything. There are even chairs around the table that might have been intended for a public sharing of their contents. Heinrich only has eyes for Natalie and does not seem curious about the documents, and neither he nor she looks at the documents at this time.

Only later that day, the papers again become the focus of attention. The fathers give their children the documents with ceremonial solemnity: "Wir gingen in den Saal. Dort gab Risach Papiere in die Hände Nataliens. Sie legte sie in die meinigen. Mein Vater gab mir auch Papiere." Again Heinrich abstains from "unveiling" the documents and returns to his room: "Ich ging in meine Wohnung, kleidete mich um und verschloß die Papiere, ohne sie anzusehen" (3:264–5). Not until after the actual wedding ceremony finalizes the union between Natalie and Heinrich they at last look at the papers and discover that both von Risach and Drendorf have given them assets beyond any expectation. In fact, it becomes apparent that Drendorf is on the same level as von Risach: "Aber auch das von dem Vater uns Übergebene war der gesammten Habe Risachs ebenbürtig, und übertraf weit meine Erwartungen" (3:279).

The climax of the competition between the fathers is the jewelry. This is a competition within the realms of aesthetics and value, which are the major focus of the novel. Already early on it becomes apparent that the topic of precious stones is a sensitive one, almost to the same degree as premature naming. It is specifically the issue of the setting that is treated with discretion. Earlier Heinrich had recounted his hesitation to initiate a conversation about this topic with the son of the jeweler: "Ich hatte aber noch immer nicht den Muth, über die gebräuchliche Fassung der Edelsteine mit ihm zu sprechen, und meine Gedanken hierüber ihm mitzutheilen" (2:61).

After the wedding, Heinrich goes back to his friend, the son of the jeweler, to thank him for the beautiful settings of the diamond and emerald pieces. It is noteworthy, first, that Heinrich thanks him specifically for the settings, as if they were the real focus of the pieces. Second, the response of his friend is one of gratitude for the involvement of von Risach and Drendorf. The jeweler feels that the aesthetic input of that type of qualitatively superior customer could advance his occupation to the level of art:

> Ich dankte ihm sehr für die prachtvolle Fassung der Diamanten und Rubinen und des Smaragdschmuckes. Er fühlte sich über Risachs und meines Vaters Urtheil sehr beglückt. "Wenn wir solche Kunden in großer Zahl hätten, wie diese zwei Männer sind, theurer Freund [...] dann würde unsere Beschäftigung bald an die Grenzen der Kunst gelangen, ja sich mit ihr vereinigen. Wir würden freudig arbeiten, und die Käufer würden erkennen, daß die geistige Arbeit auch einen Preis habe wie die Steine und das Gold" (3:277–8).

The value added by the jeweler is the connection between the stones and the gold. Ideally, the settings he creates should be as transparent as von Risach's written words in the *Dichtkunst*, where, as noted earlier, the word is not the substance of literature, but merely the carrier of thought. Similarly, the best jewelry settings are the most transparent. For example, the wedding gift from the *Fürstin* consists of a large, beautiful pearl whose setting is almost nonexistent: "Es enthielt eine einzige aber sehr große und sehr schöne Perle. Die Fassung war fast keine" (3:258). Again, this ideal of complete transparency coincides with Risach's description of poetic language.

At the end of the text both fathers have achieved ultimate beauty in their respective pieces of jewelry; this leads to what could be categorized as their sublimation. Everything seems to even out, and the fathers are elevated to a state from which they are ready to be succeeded by Heinrich, who is heir to both.

Conclusion

Der Nachsommer deals only implicitly with the economic realities of bourgeois life, but, as I have demonstrated, economic practices and structures are central to the concept of aesthetics that its narrative communicates. The illusory ways in which Stifter deeconomizes his narrative result in a further integration of economic structure into his text and ultimately lead to its total economization. Specifically, Stifter's focus on an autarchic model, his rejection of both consumption and production, and his insistance on the fair-price principle are the most important examples of this tendency in *Der Nachsommer*.

The paterfamilias is clearly the founding principle of the novel. Heinrich's father endorses the idea of Heinrich as a scientist that runs contrary to the expectations of bourgeois society's pragmatism. The monopolistic, paternal structure within which Heinrich has to operate rejects the concept of credit. This rejection of credit is a safeguard against overconsumption and inflationary tendencies both in the material economy and in the realm of representation. Within the world of paternal rule, Heinrich eventually reaches a state of conformity, undermining the focus on individuality that the father's voice preaches. This is a peculiar development in light of the genre of the *Bildungsroman*, and something that warrants further investigation.

As I have pointed out, the *Rosenhaus* economy is characterized by self-sustenance. The larger economy is excluded from the narrative, yet its marginalization is a mere illusion because all of the main characters are independently wealthy and live off of interest payments from their capital. In spite of the considerable collective wealth in *Der Nachsommer*, there is minimal need-based consumption. Heinrich, for example, is advised by his father to minimize his spending and financial risk. I have suggested that the rejection of consumption muffles the effects of the inflationary forces that come into play when consumption increases in society. It is also a way of resisting a mode of uncontrolled signification that modern money brings about, especially when its scarcity becomes compromised. The focus on Risach's autarchy at the *Rosenhaus*, where utilitarian and aesthetic ideals merge in farming activities, again gives the illusion of deeconomization when, in fact, the opposite is true.

Der Nachsommer excludes industrial production. Heinrich is marginally interested but only in production processes, i.e., the transformations (translations) that take place within the walls of the factories. The activities at the *Rosenhaus* instead focus on replicating and restoring artifacts. These activities, however, do not generate a profit in the capitalist sense of the word, but only an aesthetic surplus. In addition to categorizing, cataloguing, and systematizing artifacts, the characters in the novel are trying to control nature by organizing it into preferred patterns and forms that imitate nature. The reworking of nature into a different and much refined "natural" state is favored over the original, untouched nature; this implies that the fictitious reality of the literary text is to be preferred over reality itself.

In *Der Nachsommer*, collection is the accumulation of both economic and aesthetic value. It is also an alternative to consumption because it is an investment alternative. Activities (such as acquisition, restoration, cataloguing) surrounding the collections in *Der Nachsommer* are viewed as work because they involve the creation of meaning. There is a lively exchange of artwork to achieve perfection in the *Rosenhaus* art collection, and it is important to maintain individuality – von Risach, for example, does not include marble found by anyone else in his marble collection. This insistence on individuality, in my opinion, is a form of resistance against the modern paper money economy: As the substance of money (paper) loses its meaning, money also loses its individuality, its aesthetic value, and thereby its value as a collectible.

Another factor that relates to aesthetic representation is the importance of fair pricing. Von Risach adamantly insists on paying a fair price for any artifact that he purchases. There are several examples of his retroactively compensating former owners when he discovers additional aesthetic value in a piece of art. There are also other examples that point to the importance of fair representation. By adhering to the fair-price principle, von Risach can protect artifacts from market influences, because their aesthetic and monetary values are exactly equivalent and they are not reliant on the price-setting mechanisms of the market. This is again an instance in which Stifter deeconomizes, but the effect is the opposite; by creating this transparency between aesthetic and monetary value he succeeds in simultaneously commodifying the artifacts.

In *Der Nachsommer* the characters are always waiting for something and they avoid asking questions that are deemed premature for various reasons. The strategy of delayed naming is related to this phenomenon and is a response to a semiotic crisis that arose with the development of the modern money economy. As Peter Pfeiffer has pointed out, Stifter's frequent use of the word "Ding" is a location at which conventionality of signification and individuality of naming coincide. In that sense, "Ding" becomes like money. This is also true for the empty, majestic marble hall which has the capacity to represent all things.

The *Nachsommer* narrative is ambivalent in its understanding of the concept of work. It does not encompass work in the industrial sense but generally as an activity of ease and purpose. In addition, the borders between work and non-work are blurred. Stifter develops an aesthetic of the useful as exemplified in von Risach's *Vogelwirtschaft* for which he conducts a cost-benefit analysis. For activities relating to aesthetics, work and pleasure merge into one concept. The "work-pleasure" of creating the Beautiful (for example restorations at the Sternenhof) is very different from work in the external economy. The "business" work of Heinrich's father is monotonous and boring. A negative description of work in a modern economy is not surprising in light of Stifter's explicit attempts to exclude the modern economy from his text. By employing a "modern" time orientation within the *Rosenhaus* economy, Stifter creates a sense of urgency and significance regarding the work-pleasures that take place there. It is a way of equating the importance of aesthetic production with that of industrial production.

An accurate rendering of reality is paramount in *Der Nachsommer*. Heinrich is not a great artist, but he compensates for his aesthetic shortcomings trying to capture reality accurately. Eustach's drawings include imperfections as well, but here the deficiencies are attributed to imperfections in the original. In Heinrich's eyes, these flaws only enhance the representational quality of Eustach's drawings. The opposite of these realistic depictions is the affected and tacky display of plaster statues by the former owner of the marble statue in Italy: The plaster statues connote *Schwulst* and they give rise to an inflation of sorts because solid quality art is being undermined by the proliferation of deceptive copies.

At the end of *Der Nachsommer* there is a ceremony of opening the accounting books. A series of competitions take place between the fathers (culminating in the contest over the setting of the jewelry which are presented to Natalie) but these competitions always end in a tie. Thereby the fathers are elevated to a state which they are ready to cede to Heinrich, who is heir to both. Consequently Heinrich reaches this very position in which complete individuality coincides with complete conventionality – he assimilates both fathers and acquires features that are characteristic of money's representational capacity. Like the word "Ding" he takes on modern money's endless capability of signification.

Conclusion

> Literature has always regarded money (and the new media in any case) with distrust. Indeed, rivalry rules the relationship between the media of money and literature […]. The rivalry between money and literature is of the closest, almost sibling-like proximity. The zenith of paper money and the zenith of literature in the epoch of the educated and prosperous middle class are of a piece (Hörisch, 70–1).

As I have demonstrated there is an almost incestuous relationship between money and literature. In society, money speaks clearly and loudly, and its discourse and representational structure form philosophical and literary thought. The language of commodities "speaks ventriloquistically, as it were, through the mouths of theologians, poets, and philosophers" (Shell, 4). The two novels I have used as examples in my economopoetic study originated during the zenith of economic change in the mid-1800s.

In my inquiry, I have shown how economopoetics play a role in the two novels on three different levels, specifically as pertaining to content, representational issues, and as a literary strategy. *Soll und Haben* is set in a bourgeois capitalist environment and explicitly thematizes business and economics.

As part of his literary strategy, the author poeticizes the bourgeois economy. The principle of his economopoetics is dichotomization. By simplistically dichotomizing the material and poetic economies of the bourgeois and Jewish societies, Freytag marginalizes all systems that do not comply with the economopoetic ideals of the bourgeois economy. This leads to a certain level of bias and exclusion in his realism because he compromises his claim to depicting reality realistically.

Stifter's economopoetics works differently from Freytag's, because Stifter does not engage with the economic on the content level. Instead, he attempts to exclude it from his narrative, but in doing so, he economizes everything. The principle of total economization is the main economopoetic component in *Der Nachsommer*. The fact that Stifter is not able to escape economic implications in his narrative in spite of his efforts to remove everything relating to the modern economy from his text bespeaks the importance of this economopoetic approach.

The intersection of the material and poetic economies in *Soll und Haben* and *Der Nachsommer* is significant because economic structures and forms of representation define its aesthetic principles. The two novels diverge greatly in the ways in which they employ the economic in their narratives. *Soll und Haben* explicitly deals with themes that revolve around business and economics. In addition, Freytag creates a connection between the poetic and the economic in his preferred bourgeois economy. Undeniably, he actively employs an economopoetic model in order to promote his ideology. There is a close integration of economic thought into the narrative. For example, in his treatment of characters, Freytag relies on the structural framework of money (gold versus paper) to define the favorable traits of his protagonist, Anton Wohlfart, both in the realm of economics and aesthetics. The ideal mode of (realist) textualization is closely linked to this character and to the bourgeois economy as a whole. Also, the anti-Semitic overtones in *Soll und Haben* stem from economopoetic differences in Freytag's presentation of the diverging business behaviors of the Jews and the "German" bourgeoisie.

In *Der Nachsommer* there are fewer overt relationships between economics and poetics. Its contents are removed from the realm of economics and, in fact, Stifter distances himself from the real economy by presenting a reclusive autarchy, the *Rosenhaus*, as the prime site of aesthetics. Stifter actively tries to render the economy invisible by treating issues relating to money, business, and the economy merely as "dormant" participants. However, through principles such as autarchic existence, the importance of paying a fair price, the economization of time, and the prevalence of the *rentier* existence Stifter manages to include significant economic structures in his narrative. In spite of Stifter's insistance to ban the economic, these content clusters undermine his attempts to deeconomize *Der Nachsommer*.

The multi-faceted rejection of consumption is an important aspect of *Der Nachsommer* because it constitutes a criticism of the modern money economy and its tendencies towards overconsumption and inflated representation. It surfaces, for example, through the rejection of credit. Money created through credit increases money supply (and the means to consume) and therefore adds inflationary pressures to the economy. In *Soll und Haben* there is a similar tendency to exclude consumption from the narrative and also to reject credit. As I have shown, these tendencies function differently in *Der Nachsommer* and *Soll und Haben*. In *Der Nachsommer* they are an expressed skepticism against the modern money economy and its destabilizing impact on the realm of both material and poetic representation, whereas in *Soll und Haben* consumption and commodity exchange are opposing concepts. In the economopoetics of *Soll und Haben*, both play into the dichotomization that Freytag sets up between the bourgeois and Jewish economies.

The concept of work is relevant to both texts, and in both cases the authors present a nontraditional notion of work. The whole realm of industrial work has been excluded from both novels. Stifter focuses on the "work-pleasures" of the aesthetic activities that take place at the *Rosenhaus* and *Sternenhof* which he contrasts to work in the external economy as exemplified in Heinrich's father's monotonous business activities. Freytag, on the other hand, surrounds the work of the bourgeois merchant with an aura of poesy. He presents the bourgeois economy as the primary site for poetic experience and the prime source of literary production. The interconnectedness between the participants in Freytag's commodity exchange makes his bourgeois economy "textual."

Another parallel between the two novels is the way in which the protagonists, Anton and Heinrich, arrive at a state of complete assimilation to the ideals of the patriarchal systems within which they operate. The educational process promotes conformity. I have argued that both characters experience a loss of individuality. In Anton's case his character is flattened to the point at which he becomes a completely neutral mediator of exchange, and, in essence, money. Even though Anton's "development" is described in positive terms in *Soll und Haben*, there is a disconcerting moment of destruction at the end of the novel when he is subsumed by the pages of the *Geheimbuch*. Heinrich's case is more complicated, because the *Nachsommer* narrative unfailingly promotes individuality, but at the same time allows Heinrich to become completely conventional as he assimilates to the paternal ideal. This tension between absolute individuality and conventionality is yet another example of how economic structures come into play in *Der Nachsommer*. Heinrich's complete assimilation equates his position with that of money, because of its eternal capacity to signify. This openness to signification, in turn, negates individuality.

The tendency towards assimilation in both novels is interesting in light of the tradition of the *Bildungsroman*. We see the young protagonists reach a state of assimilation and conformity. This is a reversal of the traditional *Bildungsroman* and an interesting element that my economopoetic analysis of the novels has brought to the fore. The ambivalence between individuality and conventionality relates to economic structures in which these two extremes converge in money. I have used a different conceptual framework in my interpretation of *Soll und Haben* and *Der Nachsommer*, but in the future it would be fruitful to explore their economopoetics within the genre of the *Bildungsroman*.

My interpretation demonstrates how the main poetical strategies of the two novels, dichotomization (*Soll und Haben*) and total economization (*Der Nachsommer*), are defined by economic themes, structures, and forms. Although very different in their treatment of topics relating to business and economics, both texts employ economic thought in their narratives. The diverging patterns of economopoetics are central commentaries on the underlying realist aesthetics.

Ultimately, the investigation of economopoetics sheds light on the limitations of realist representation as presented in these two literary works. As I have shown in the previous chapters, both Freytag and Stifter are ambivalent in their preference of realist representation. This ambivalence is connected with the move to a more abstract and symbolic representation in the money economy through the increasing circulation of paper money at the time. Both novels address issues relating to the changing money economy, albeit in different ways. Freytag's economopoetic dichotomization leads to a state of exclusion which undermines his realism. Stifter's total economization, in turn, undermines his realist model that attempts to exclude the economic. In this difference rests an important finding of my study, i.e., that in spite of money's apparent absence from the core content of some literary texts, structurally, it is difficult to avoid.

The two novels are located at the extremes of the spectrum of realist literature and economopoetics alike: *Soll und Haben* aestheticizes the economic, *Der Nachsommer* economizes the aesthetic. By showing the economopoetic connections in a text like *Der Nachsommer*, which ultimately seeks to exclude everything relating to the economy from its narrative, it is reasonable to assume that it would be productive to investigate the economopoetics of additional texts. While I am not proposing that my approach of using economopoetics to interpret literature has a universal application, my investigation of *Der Nachsommer* implies that the study of economopoetics can be relevant to a broad range of literature, even that which does *not* explicitly thematize money and economics. Economic organizing principles still inform and enrich the literary interpretations of such texts.

Bibliography

Achinger, Christine. "Prosa der Verhältnisse und der Poesie der Ware: Versöhnte Moderne und Realismus in *Soll und Haben*", *150 Jahre* Soll und Haben*: Studien zu Gustav Freytags kontroversem Roman*. Ed. Florian Krobb. Würzburg: Königshausen & Neumann, 2005. 67–86.

Albrecht, Wolfgang. "Geschäft, Genuss, Gemeinnutz: Korrelationen und Traditionen der ästhetisierten Lebens-Ordnung in Stifters *Nachsommer*." *Michigan Germanic Studies* 18 (1992): 1–18.

Bark, Joachim. "Bildungsromane." *Deutsche Literatur: Eine Sozialgeschichte 7: Vom Nachmärz zur Gründerzeit: Realismus 1848–1880*. Ed. Horst Albert Glaser. Reinbek bei Hamburg: Rowohlt, 1982. 144–62.

Beaton, Kenneth Bruce. "Gustav Freytag, Julian Schmidt und die Romantheorie nach der Revolution von 1848." *Jahrbuch der Raabe-Gesellschaft* (1976): 7–32.

Belgum, Kirsten L. "High Historicism and Narrative Restoration: The Seamless Interior of Adalbert Stifter's *Nachsommer*." *Germanic Review* 67 (1992): 15–25.

Berman, Russell. *The Rise of the Modern German Novel: Crisis and Charisma*. Cambridge, Mass.: Harvard University Press, 1986.

Bernd, C.A. "The Advent of German Poetic Realism." *Formen realistischer Erzählkunst: Festschrift for Charlotte Jolles*. Ed. Jörg Thunecke. Nottingham: Sherwood, 1979. 14–23.

Blackall, Eric A. *Adalbert Stifter: A Critical Study*. Cambridge: Cambridge University Press, 1948.

Blackbourn, David. *The Long Nineteenth Century: A History of Germany 1780–1918*. New York: Oxford University Press, 1998.

Blackbourn, David, and Geoff Eley. *The Peculiarities of German History: Bourgeois Society and Politics in Nineteenth-Century Germany*. Oxford: Oxford University Press, 1984.

Blasberg, Cornelia. *Erschriebene Tradition: Adalbert Stifter oder das Erzählen im Zeichen verlorener Geschichten.* Freiburg: Rombach, 1998.

Bräutigam, Bernd. "Candide im Comptoir: Zur Bedeutung der Poesie in Gustav Freytags *Soll und Haben.*" *Germanisch-Romanische Monatsschrift* 35 (1985): 395–411.

Brinkmann, Richard, ed. *Begriffsbestimmung des literarischen Realismus.* Darmstadt: Wissenschaftliche Buchgesellschaft, 1987.

Buckley, Thomas. *Nature, Science, Realism: A Re-examination of Programmatic Realism and the Works of Adalbert Stifter and Gottfried Keller.* New York: Peter Lang, 1995.

Bullivant, Keith. "Realismus und Romanästhetik: Überlegungen zu einem problematischen Aspekt der deutschen Literatur." *Orbis Litterarum* 39 (1984): 1–13.

Carter, T.E. "Freytag's *Soll und Haben*: A Liberal National Manifesto as a Best-Seller." *German Life and Letters* 21 (1968): 320–29.

Chown, John. *A History of Money from AD 800.* London: Routledge and the Institute of Economic Affairs, 1994.

Craig, Gordon. *The Germans.* New York: Putman, 1982.

Davies, Glyn. *A History of Money: From Ancient Times to the Present Day.* Cardiff: University of Wales Press, 1994.

Denkler, Horst. "Die Schule des Kapitalismus. Reinhold Solgers deutsch-amerikanisches Seitenstück zu Gustav Freytags *Soll und Haben.*" *Amerika in der deutschen Literatur.* Ed. Sigrid Bauschinger, Horst Denkler and Wilfried Malsch. Stuttgart: Philipp Reclam, 1975. 108–23.

Downing, Eric. "Adalbert Stifter and the Scope of Realism." *Germanic Review* 74 (1999): 229–41.

Eicher, Thomas. "Poesie, Poetisierung und Poetizität in Gustav Freytags *Soll und Haben.*" *Wirkendes Wort: Deutsche Sprache und Literatur in Forschung und Lehren.* 45 (1995): 64–81.

Eisele, Ulf. "Realismus-Theorie." *Deutsche Literatur: Eine Sozialgeschichte 7: Vom Nachmärz zur Gründerzeit: Realismus 1848–1880.* Ed. Horst Albert Glaser. Reinbek: Rowohlt, 1982. 36–46.

——. *Die Struktur des modernen deutschen Romans.* Tübingen: Niemeyer, 1984.

——. *Realismus und Ideologie: Zur Kritik der literarischen Theorie nach 1848 am Beispiel des "Deutschen Museums."* Stuttgart: Metzler, 1976.

Fontane, Theodor. "Rezension zu Gustav Freytags *Soll und Haben*." *Realismus und Gründerzeit: Manifeste und Dokumente zur deutschen Literatur 1848–1880.* 2. Ed. Max Bucher et al. Stuttgart: Metzler, 1975. 328–36.

Fraser, L.M. *Economic Thought and Language.* Norwich: Empire Press, 1947.

Freytag, Gustav. *Soll und Haben.* Leipzig: Hirzel, 1901.

Gabriel, Hans P. "Prescribing Reality: The Preface as a Device of Literary Realism in Auerbach, Keller and Stifter." *Colloquia Germanica* 32 (1999): 325–44.

Gall, Lothar. *Bürgertum in Deutschland.* (1989) Berlin: Goldmann, 1996.

Gelber, Mark H. "Die literarische Umwelt zu Gustav Freytags *Soll und Haben* und die Realismustheorie der Grenzboten." *Orbis Litterarum* 39 (1984): 38–53.

Geulen, Eva. "Depicting Description: Lukács and Stifter." *Germanic Review* 73 (1998): 267–79.

——. *Worthörig wider Willen: Darstellungsproblematik und Sprachreflexion in der Prosa Adalbert Stifters.* Munich: Iudicium, 1992.

Glaser, Horst Albert. *Die Restauration des Schönen: Stifters* Nachsommer. Stuttgart: Metzler, 1965

Goux, Jean-Joseph. *Symbolic Economies: After Marx and Freud.* Trans. Jennifer Curtiss Gage. Ithaca: Cornell University Press, 1990.

Gray, Richard. *Stations of the Divided Subject: Contestation and Ideological Legitimation in German Bourgeois Literature 1770–1914.* Stanford: Stanford University Press, 1995.

Griffiths, Elystan. "A Nation of Provincials? German Identity in Gustav Freytags Novel *Die Ahnen* (1872–80)." *Monatshefte* 96 (2004): 220–33.

Groseclose, Elgin. *Money and Man: A Survey of Monetary Experience.* Norman: University of Oklahoma Press, 1976.

Grunert, Mark. "Lenore oder die Versuchung des Bürgers: Romantischer 'Zauber' und realistische Ideologie in Gustav Freytags *Soll und Haben*." *Monatshefte* 85 (1993): 134–52.

Gubser, Martin. *Literarischer Antisemitismus: Untersuchungen zu Gustav Freytag und anderen bürgerlichen Schriftstellern des 19. Jahrhunderts.* Göttingen: Wallstein, 1998.

Häntzschel, Günter. "Adalbert Stifters Nausikaa." *Stifter-Studien.* Ed. Walter Hettche et al. Tübingen: Niemeyer, 2000. 87–96.

Hettche, Walter. "'Dichten' oder 'Machen'? Adalbert Stifters Arbeit an seinem Roman *Der Nachsommer*." *Stifter-Studien*. Ed. Walter Hettche et al. Tübingen: Niemeyer. 2000. 75–86.

Hobsbawm, Eric J. "Kultur und Geschlecht im europäischen Bürgertum 1870–1914." *Bürgerinnen und Bürger: Geschlechterverhältnisse im 19. Jahrhundert.* Ed. Ute Frevert. Göttingen: Vandenhoeck & Ruprecht, 1988. 175–89.

Hohendahl, Peter Uwe. "Literaturkritik und Literaturgeschichte." *Deutsche Literatur: Eine Sozialgeschichte 7: Vom Nachmärz zur Gründerzeit: Realismus 1848–1880.* Ed. Horst Albert Glaser. Reinbek: Rowohlt, 1982. 47–58.

Holub, Robert. *Reflections of Realism: Paradox, Norm, and Ideology in Nineteenth-Century German Prose.* Detroit: Wayne State University Press, 1991.

Hörisch, Jochen. "Äquivalenzen, Gleichgültigkeiten, Ringe: Das Geld der Literatur." *Merkur* 50 (1996): 127–37.

——. *Heads or Tails: The Poetics of Money.* Trans. Amy Horning Marschall. Detroit: Wayne State University Press, 2000.

Hubrich, Peter Heinz. *Gustav Freytags "Deutsche Ideologie" in* Soll und Haben. Kronberg: Scriptor, 1974.

Jameson, Fredric. *Postmodernism, or, The Cultural Logic of Late Capitalism.* Durham: Duke University Press, 1991

Kaiser, Nancy. *Social Integration and Narrative Structure. Patterns of Realism in Auerbach, Freytag, Fontane, and Raabe.* New York: Peter Lang, 1986.

Kaplan, Marion. "Freizeit-Arbeit: Geschlechterräume im deutsch-jüdischen Bürgertum 1870–1914." *Bürgerinnen und Bürger: Geschlechterverhältnisse im 19. Jahrhundert.* Ed. Ute Frevert. Göttingen: Vandenhoeck & Ruprecht, 1988. 157–74.

Kars, Gustav. *Das Bild des Juden in der deutschen Literatur des 18. und 19. Jahrhunderts.* Freiburg: Burg-Verlag Literaturwissenschaft, 1988.

Keenan, Thomas. "The Point is to (Ex)Change It: Reading Capital, Rhetorically." *Fetishism as Cultural Discourse.* Ed. Emily Apter and William Pietz. Ithaca: Cornell University Press, 1993.

Kienzle, Michael. *Der Erfolgsroman.* Stuttgart: Metzler, 1975.

Kohl, Stephan. *Realismus: Theorie und Geschichte.* Munich: Fink, 1977.

Köhnke, Klaus Christian. "Ein antisemitischer Autor wider Willen: Zu Gustav Freytags Roman *Soll und Haben.*" *Conditio Judaica: Judentum, Antisemitismus und deutschsprachige Literatur vom 18. Jahrhundert bis zum ersten Weltkrieg.* Ed. Hans-Otto Horch and Horst Denkler. Vol. 2. Tübingen: Niemeyer, 1989. 130–47.

Krohn, Claus-Dieter. "Epoche—Sozialgeschichtlicher Abriß." *Deutsche Literatur: Eine Sozialgeschichte 7: Vom Nachmärz zur Gründerzeit: Realismus 1848–1880.* Ed. Horst Albert Glaser. Reinbek: Rowohlt, 1982. 11–23.

Lachinger, Johann. "Adalbert Stifters *Nachsommer*: Ein singuläres episches Werk." *Stifter-Studien.* Ed. Walter Hettche et al. Tübingen: Niemeyer, 2000. 97–100.

Lindau, Marie-Ursula. *Stifters* Nachsommer*: Ein Roman der verhaltenen Rührung*. Bern: Franke, 1974.

Lonner, Alyssa A. *Mediating the Past. Gustav Freytag, Progress, and German Historical Identity, 1848–1871.* New York: Peter Lang, 2005.

Lukács, Georg. *Essays über Realismus*. Neuwied: Luchterhand, 1971.

Mayer, Gerhart. "Adalbert Stifters *Nachsommer*: Gestaltbegriff und Werkstruktur." *Formen realistischer Erzählkunst: Festschrift for Charlotte Jolles.* Ed. Jörg Thunecke. Nottingham: Sherwood, 1979. 120–27.

McInnes, E. "Die Poesie des Geschäfts: Social Analysis and Polemic in *Soll und Haben.*" *Formen realistischer Erzählkunst: Festschrift for Charlotte Jolles.* Ed. Jörg Thunecke. Nottingham: Sherwood, 1979. 99–107.

McIsaac, Peter M. "The Museal Path to Bildung: Collecting, Exhibiting and Exchange in Stifter's *Der Nachsommer*." *German Life and Letters* 57 (2004): 268–89.

Michaels, Walter Benn. *The Gold Standard and the Logic of Naturalism: American Literature at the Turn of the Century*. Berkeley: University of California Press, 1987.

Minden, M.R. "The Place of Inheritance in the Bildungsroman." *Deutsche Vierteljahresschrift* 57 (1983): 33–63.

Moore, Carl, und Alvin Russell. *Money: Its Origin, Development and Modern Use*. Jefferson: McFarland, 1987.

Müller, Klaus-Detlef. *Bürgerlicher Realismus: Grundlagen und Interpretationen*. Königstein: Athenäum, 1981.

Ottel, Fritz. *Ständische Theorie des Geldes*. Jena: Gustav Fischer, 1934.

Pazi, Margarita. "Wie gleicht man auch ethisch *Soll und Haben* aus?" *Zeitschrift für Deutsche Philologie* 106 (1987): 198–218.

Pfeiffer, Peter C. "Adalbert Stifter's Money Thing." *History, Text, Value: Essays on Adalbert Stifter*. Londoner Symposium 2003. Ed. Michael Minden, Martin Swales, and Godela Weiss-Sussex. London: School of Advanced Studies, University of London (2006): 80–6.

——. "Den Tod aus dem Bereich des Romans fernhalten: Zur ästhetischen Funktion des Todes in der Literatur des bürgerlichen Realismus." *Germanic Review* 70 (1995): 15–23.

——. "Tod, Entstellung, Hässlichkeit: Fontanes, Schach von Wuthenow." *Zeitschrift für Deutsche Philologie* 113 (1994): 264–76.

Pfotenhauer, Helmut. "Bild und Schrift: Zur Funktion von Medienwechseln in der realistischen Literatur: Stifter, Keller." *Das schwierige neunzehnte Jahrhundert*. Ed. Jürgen Barkhoff et al. Tübingen: Niemeyer, 2000. 207–27.

Ping, Larry L. *Gustav Freytag and the Prussian Gospel. Novels, Liberalism, and History*. New York: Peter Lang, 2006.

Poggi, Gianfranco. *Money and the Mind*. Berkeley: University of California Press, 1993.

Ragg-Kirby, Helena. *Adalbert Stifter's Late Prose: The Mania for Moderation*. Rochester: Camden House, 2000.

——. "'Eine immerwährende Umwandlung der Ansichten': Narrators and Their Perspectives in the Works of Adalbert Stifter." *Language Review* 95 (2000): 127–43.
Ridley, Hugh. "Zwischen Anstand und Ästetik: Zu sozialen und literarischen Codes in Gustav Freytags *Soll und Haben*." *Zeitschrift für Germanistik* 11 (2001): 105–16.
Riegel, Klaus. *Foundations of Dialectical Psychology.* New York: Academic Press, 1979.
Rindisbacher, Hans J. "From National Task to Individual Pursuit: The Poetics of Work in Freytag, Stifter, and Raabe." *A Companion to German Realism 1848–1900.* Ed. Todd Kontje. Rochester, NY: Camden House, 2002 183–221.
——. *The Smell of Books: A Cultural-Historical Study of Olfactory Perception in Literature.* Ann Arbor: University of Michigan Press, 1992.
Rotenstreich, Nathan. *Reflection and Action.* Dordrecht: Nijhoff, 1985.
Russell, Norman. *The Novelist and Mammon: Literary Responses to the World of Commerce in the Nineteenth Century.* Oxford: Clarendon Press, 1986.
Sagarra, Eda. *Germany in the Nineteenth Century: History and Literature.* New York: Peter Lang, 2001.
Salm, Carola. *Reale und symbolische Ordnungen in Stifters* Nachsommer. Frankfurt a.M.: Peter Lang, 1991.
Schmidt, Sabine. "Adalbert Stifters *Nachsommer*: Subjektive Idealität: Heinrich Drendorfs Subjektkonstitution im Spiegel seiner Selbstdefinition." *Geschlecht—Literatur—Geschichte*, I. Ed. Gudrun Loster-Schneider. St. Ingbert: Rohrig, 1999. 81–104.
Schneider, Michael. *Geschichte als Gestalt: Formen der Wirklichkeit und Wirklichkeit der Form in Gustav Freytag' Roman* "Soll und Haben." Stuttgart: Heinz, 1980.
Shell, Marc. *The Economy of Literature.* (1978) Baltimore: Softshell, 1993.
——. *Money, Language and Thought.* (1982) Baltimore: Softshell, 1993.
Simmel, Georg. *Philosophie des Geldes.* (1900) Frankfurt a.M.: Suhrkamp. 1989.

Sjögren, Christine. "The Equivocal Light of the Marmorsaal: Traces of Mysticism in Stifter's Novel, *Der Nachsommer*." *Journal of English and Germanic Philology* 69 (1970): 108–17.

——. *The Marble Statue as Idea: Collected Essays on Adalbert Stifter's* "Der Nachsommer." Chapel Hill: University of North Carolina Press, 1972.

Smith, Woodruff. *Politics and the Sciences of Culture in Germany 1840–1920*. New York: Oxford University Press, 1991.

Sprenger, Bernd. *Das Geld der Deutschen: Geldgeschichte Deutschlands von den Anfängen bis zur Gegenwart*. Paderborn: Schöningh, 1991.

Steinecke, Hartmut. "Gustav Freytags *Soll und Haben*—ein 'realistischer' Roman?" *Formen realistischer Erzählkunst: Festschrift for Charlotte Jolles*. Ed, Jörg Thunecke. Nottingham: Sherwood, 1979. 108–19.

Stern, J.P. *Idylls and Realities: Studies in Nineteenth-Century German Literature*. New York: Ungar, 1971.

Stifter, Adalbert. *Adalbert Stifter Werke und Briefe: Historisch-Kritische Gesamtausgabe*. Ed. Wolfgang Frühwald & Walter Hettche. Stuttgart: Kohlhammer, 1997–2000.

——. *Über unsere gegenwärtige Lage und unsere sittliche Verbesserung in Adalbert Stifter*. Gesammelte Werke. Frankfurt: Inselverlag, 1959.

Stockinger, Ludwig. "Realpolitik, Realismus und das Ende des bürgerlichen Wahrheitsanspruchs: Überlegungen zur Funktion des programmatischen Realismus am Beispiel von Gustav Freytags *Soll und Haben*." *Bürgerlicher Realismus: Grundlagen und Interpretationen*. Ed. Klaus-Detlef Müller. Königstein: Athenäum, 1981. 174–202.

Swales, Martin, and Erika Swales. *Adalbert Stifter: A Critical Study*. London: Cambridge University Press, 1984.

Thomas, Lionel. "Bourgeois Attitudes: Gustav Freytag's Novels of Life in Nineteenth-Century Germany." *Proceedings of the Leeds Philosophical and Literary Society, Literary and Historical Section*. 1973. 59–74.

Vernon, John. *Money and Fiction: Literary Realism in the Nineteenth and Early Twentieth Centuries.* Ithaca: Cornell University Press, 1984.

Vilar, Pierre. *A History of Gold and Money 1450–1920.* London: NLB, 1976.

Vosskamp, Wilhelm. *Romantheorie in Deutschland: Von Martin Opitz bis Friedrich von Blanckenburg.* Stuttgart: Metzler, 1973.

Wagner, Karl. "Patriarchalisches Stilleben? Ein sozialgeschichtlicher Versuch über Stifters *Nachsommer.*" *Adalbert Stifter Institut des Landes Oberösterreich: Vierteljahresschrift* 29 (1980): 139–65.

Weatherford, Jack. *The History of Money: From Sandstone to Cyberspace.* New York: Crown Publishers, 1997.

Weiss, Jochen. "Die protestantische Ethik und der Geist der Buchführung: Bürgerliche Lebensbilanz in *Soll und Haben.*" *150 Jahre* Soll und Haben*: Studien zu Gustav Freytags kontroversem Roman.* Ed. Florian Krobb. Würzburg: Königshausen & Neumann, 2005. 87–101.

Index

accumulation 25, 31n9, 49, 55, 60, 120, 125–6, 136, 160
Achinger, Christine 93n34
antiaristocratic 28
anti-Polish 28
anti-Semitic 28, 30n7, 164
aristocratic 28–9, 31–2, 53, 55n22, 61n25, 63, 66–7, 82, 90n32, 92n33, 93–4, 96
art 12n4, 14–15, 22–4, 24n18, 62, 75, 83–4, 101–2, 111n11, 115, 118–20, 123, 126, 128, 130, 139, 144–9, 152, 154–6, 158, 160–2
art of representation 14
autarchy 107, 110–113, 127, 131, 160, 164

Beaton, Kenneth 56n23
Belgum, Kirsten 113n13, 115n14
Benn Michaels, Walter 16n8
Berman, Russell 17n9, 22–3n16, 29n4–5, 31n9, 32n10, 35, 36n13, 43n15, 48–9, 55n22, 59n24, 60–1, 61n25, 90n32, 91, 92n33, 143–6
Blackall, Eric 106n9, 118n15
Blackbourn, David 121n16
Blasberg, Cornelia 121, 121n17
bookkeeping 32, 66, 69–70, 69n27, 74–5, 78–9, 95–6, 102, 104
bourgeois
  capitalism 48, 88, 89
  capitalist 47–8, 50, 55n22, 56, 89–90, 94, 96, 98, 107, 163
  ideals 42, 58, 79, 81
  merchant 15, 32, 37, 52, 56, 63, 66–7, 69n27, 93, 165
  society 51, 57, 77, 81, 84, 100, 159
Bräutigam, Bernd 46n17

capital accumulation 126, 136
Carlyle, Thomas 111n11
Carter, T.E. 28n2
circulation 20, 25, 57, 61, 95, 98, 110, 128, 166
collection/collecting 77, 98, 117, 120–7, 129–30, 135, 145, 148, 155–6, 160–1
commerce 27n1, 45, 46n17, 97–8, 98n2–3
commodity consumption (*see also* consumption) 57
commodity exchange 18, 34, 36, 39–41, 44–50, 56, 57–9, 65, 70–1, 73, 75, 82, 90, 94, 97, 98n3, 112, 125, 165
consumption 15, 25, 32, 33n11, 38, 57, 94–5, 98–9, 108–12, 120, 126–7, 132, 141, 159–60, 165
consumption abstinence 61
Craig, Gordon 16n7–8,
credit 9n1, 15, 20, 21n13, 64, 66–9, 86, 88, 95, 102, 159, 165
credit avoidance 70
"credit money" 69

debit 65–6, 86, 88, 95
destruction 62, 64, 67, 84, 165
dowries 153
drawing 79, 114, 119, 143–5, 154, 162

economic
  crisis 112
  power 21
  life 56n23, 82
  verbal representation, and 12
economopoetic 17–20, 23n16, 24–5, 29, 31, 38–9, 43, 55, 61, 73n28, 76, 84, 89, 93–4, 96, 98–9, 128, 131, 163–7

economy
aristocratic 28, 82, 93
bourgeois 12n4, 18, 31–2, 35–6, 38, 41, 43, 45–7, 50, 54–8, 60, 62, 65, 68–9, 75–6, 77, 81–2, 86, 88, 93–4, 101, 163–5
capitalist 107, 111, 116, 126, 133, 141
closed 110–11
market 99–100, 110, 112, 128, 130–1, 142
material 19, 27, 29, 65, 95, 97–8, 107–8, 159
merchant 50n19, 71, 93
modern 51n21, 125, 141, 143, 161–2, 164
paper 24
poetic 16–19, 24–5, 27–9, 32, 37, 39, 43, 47, 65, 82–3, 93, 95, 98, 163–4
Eicher, Thomas 44n16, 154
Eisele, Ulf 22n15
ethic 28, 50n20, 59, 118n15
exchange 9–10, 12–13, 15, 18, 20, 25, 29–30, 32, 34, 36–7, 39–42, 44–48, 49–50, 53, 56, 57–61, 64–5, 70–1, 73–5, 82, 84, 89–90, 93–4, 96, 97–9, 106, 109, 112, 123, 125, 128, 131–2, 155, 160, 165

financial risk 55, 108
Fontane, Theodor 13, 23

Gabriel, Hans P. 148
Gelber, Mark 73n28
Geulen, Eva 150n22
Goux, Jean-Joseph 17, 18n11, 104, 105n7
Gray, Richard T. 10, 12n4
Grunert, Mark 79n29

Holub, Robert 21, 23n17, 24n18, 119–20, 145, 151–2
Hörisch, Jochen 9n1, 10, 15n5, 17n11, 97n2, 109n10, 163

idealist philosophy 13
industrial production 49–50, 56, 57, 98, 100, 113, 136, 143, 160, 162
Industrial Revolution 15, 20
industrial society 113–14
industriousness 28
inflation 13, 69, 95, 109, 134, 136, 147, 159–60, 162, 165
inheritance 107, 130, 141, 153–5
investment 15, 21n13, 120, 126–7, 160

Jackson, Paul 49n19
jewelry 108–9, 158–9, 162

Köhnke, Klaus Christian 28n3

literary realism 16, 18–19, 23n16, 148
Lonner, Alyssa 34n12

McInnes, E. 30n6, 48n18, 56n23, 67n26
McIsaac, Peter 124n18
mediating commodity 88
mediator
of exchange 37, 90, 95–6
neutral 31n9, 41, 57, 64, 84, 89–90, 94, 96, 165
mentoring relationship 84
Mephistopheles 13
middle-class 12n4, 21, 34n12, 163
Minden, M.R. 154–5
money
coins 10, 12, 17, 20, 43, 69, 97
electronic 10, 17
facilitator of exchange 132, 155
gold coins 10, 16, 62, 83, 148
paper 10, 11n2–3, 13–16, 18n11, 19, 21, 24n19, 62, 69, 83, 95, 109n10, 110, 111n11, 118, 125, 148, 161, 163, 166
social bond 9, 20

money-lending 42
Müller, Klaus-Detlev 99n4, 104n6

"naturalness" 36, 40, 93, 116, 149

orderliness 28, 100, 116, 137
overconsumption 102, 111, 131, 159, 165

painting 123, 127–9, 143–5
Pazi, Margarita 28n3
Pfeiffer, Peter 83, 90n31, 109–10, 126, 128, 133–4, 141–2, 161
Pfotenhauer, Helmut 21
Ping, Larry L. 30n7
"poetic plots" 15
Poetic Realism 17, 21, 22n15, 23, 24n18, 29, 35, 87, 115, 150
preservation 25
production 12–13, 21, 22n15, 23, 25, 21, 48, 49–50, 54, 56, 57, 94, 96, 98, 110, 113–16, 118, 127, 131, 141, 143, 144, 147, 159–60, 162
"productive" 112, 131

Ragg-Kirby, Helena 121–2, 149–50
reliability 28, 60
revenue 52–3, 108
Ricardo, David 100
Riegel, Klaus 11n2
Rindisbacher, Hans 30n8, 33n11, 37–8, 50n21, 59, 104, 117–18, 137n21

Sagarra, Eda 21n13
Schmidt, Sabine 46n17, 151, 156n23
sculpture 145–6
security 44, 52, 54, 86, 122
selfsustenance 107, 127, 160
Shell, Marc 10, 11n3, 12–14, 15n5, 17, 19, 163
signifier/signified 10, 13, 32n10, 53, 62, 83–4, 94, 98, 110, 117, 133–4
Simmel, Georg 16n8, 20
stability 16, 42, 48, 86, 93, 109, 113n13, 122, 155
statue 119–20, 129, 131, 145–7, 162
Steinecke, H. 20n12, 36n14, 50n20
Stern, J.P. 105n8
Swales, Martin and Erika 133n20
symbiotic 17, 17n10, 143

Thomas, Lionel 27n1

Vernon, John 10, 14–17, 20

wealth 12, 15–16, 17n9, 48, 50, 57–9, 67–9, 77, 84, 95, 107, 160
Weatherford, Jack 9n1
Weiss, Jochen 69n27

North American Studies in 19th-Century German Literature

This series of monographs is about post-Romantic literature during the 19th century in German-speaking lands. The series endeavors to embrace studies in criticism, literary history, the symbiosis with other national literatures, as well as the social and political dimensions of literature. Our aim is to offer contributions by American scholars, to renovate the reformation of the canon, the rediscovery of once significant authors, the reevaluation of texts and their contexts, and a renewed understanding and appreciation of a body of literature that was acknowledged as internationally important in the 19th century.

Vol. 44 Karin Baumgartner: Public Voices. Political Discourse in the Writings of Caroline de la Motte Fouqué. 276 pp., 2009.

Vol. 43 K. Scott Baker: Drama and "Ideenschmuggel". Inserted Performance as Communicative Strategy in Karl Gutzkow's Plays 1839–1849. 187 pp., 2008.

Vol. 42 Anna H. Helm: The Intersection of Material and Poetic Economy. Gustav Freytag's *Soll und Haben* and Adalbert Stifter's *Der Nachsommer*. 181 pp., 2009.

Vol. 41 Kim Fordham: Trials and Tribunals in the Dramas of Heinrich von Kleist. 153 pp., 2007.

Vol. 40 Marjanne E. Goozé (ed.): Challenging Separate Spheres. Female *Bildung* in Eighteenth- and Nineteenth-Century Germany. 317 pp., 2007.

Vol. 39 Arne Koch: Between National Fantasies and Regional Realities. The Paradox of Identity in Nineteenth-Century German Literature. 270 pp., 2006.

Vol. 38 Rohit Sharma: On the Seventh Solitude. Endless Becoming and Eternal Return in the Poetry of Friedrich Nietzsche. 293 pp., 2006.

Vol. 37 Larry L. Ping: Gustav Freytag and the Prussian Gospel. Novels, Liberalism, and History. 352 pp., 2006.

Vol. 36 Alyssa A. Lonner: Mediating the Past. Gustav Freytag, Progress, and German Historical Identity, 1848–1871. 255 pp., 2005.

Vol. 35 Rinske van Stipriaan Pritchett: The Art of Comedy and Social Critique in Nineteenth-Century Germany. Charlotte Birch-Pfeiffer (1800–1868). 240 pp., 2005.

Vol. 34 Helen Ferstenberg: Meditations on Jewish Creative Identity. Representations of the Jewish Artist in the Works of German-Jewish Writers from Heine to Feuchtwanger. 229 pp., 2004.

Vol. 33 Clifford Albrecht Bernd: Theodor Storm. The Dano-German Poet and Writer. 233 pp., 2003, 2005.

Vol. 32 Edward Mornin: Through Alien Eyes. The Visit of the Russian Ship *Rurik* to San Francisco in 1816 and the Men behind the Visit. 125 pp., 2002.

Vol. 31 Karin Kluger: Der letzte Augenblick der hübschen Idylle. Die Problematisierung der Idylle bei Wilhelm Raabe. 199 pp., 2001.

Vol. 30 Christine Geffers Browne: Theodor Storm. Das Spannungsverhältnis zwischen Glauben und Aberglauben in seinen Novellen. 155 pp., 2002.

Vol. 29 Vanessa Van Ornam: Fanny Lewald and Nineteenth-Century Constructions of Femininity. 192 pp., 2002.

Vol. 28 Jennifer Cizik Marshall: Betrothal, Violence, and the "Beloved Sacrifice" in Nineteenth-Century German Literature. 265 pp., 2001.

Vol. 27 Lisabeth M. Hock: Replicas of a Female Prometheus. The Textual Personae of Bettina von Arnim. 260 pp., 2001.

Vol. 26 Lorie A. Vanchena: Political Poetry in Periodicals and the Shaping of German National Consciousness in the Nineteenth Century. 290 pp., 2000.

Vol. 25 Jerry Schuchalter: Narratives of America and the Frontier in Nineteenth-Century German Literature. 302 pp., 2000.

Vol. 24 Michael Boehringer: The Telling Tactics of Narrative Strategies in Tieck, Kleist, Stifter, and Storm. 204 pp., 1999.

Vol. 23 Christine Anton: Selbstreflexivität der Kunsttheorie in den Künstlernovellen des Realismus. 227 pp., 1998.

Vol. 22 James M. McGlathery: Wagner's Operas and Desire. 312 pp., 1998.

Vol. 20 Peter O. Arnds: Wilhelm Raabe's "Der Hungerpastor" and Charles Dickens's "David Copperfield". 202 pp., 1997.

Vol. 19 Diana Lynn Justis: The Feminine in Heine's Life and Oeuvre. Self and Other. 247 pp., 1997.

Vol. 18 Rodney R. Taylor : Perspectives on Spinoza in Works by Schiller, Büchner, and C.F. Meyer. Five Essays. 170 pp., 1995.

Vol. 17 Nancy Birch Wagner: Goethe as Cultural Icon. Intertextual Encounters with Stifter and Fontane. 220 pp., 1994.

Vol. 15 Helen G. Morris-Keitel: Identity in Transition. The Images of Working-Class Women in Social Prose of the "Vormärz" (1840–1848). 216 pp., 1995.

Vol. 14 Henry H. H. Remak: Structural Elements of the German Novella from Goethe to Thomas Mann. 341 pp., 1996, 2001.

Vol. 13 Tamara Felden: Frauen Reisen. Zur literarischen Repräsentation weiblicher Geschlechterrollenerfahrung im 19. Jahrhundert. 179 pp., 1993.

Vol. 12 Charles F. Good: Domination, Dependence, Denial and Despair. Father-Daughter Relationships in Grillparzer, Hebbel and Hauptmann. 175 pp., 1993.

Vol. 11 David L. Dysart: The Role of the Painting in the Works of Theodor Storm. 1992

Vol. 10 John Carson Pettey: Nietzsche's Philosophical and Narrative Styles. 1992.

Vol. 9 Beth L. Mugge-Meiburg: Words Chiseled into Marble. Artworks in the Prose Narratives of Conrad Ferdinand Meyer. 1991.

Vol. 8 Mark Lehrer: Intellektuelle Aporie und literarische Originalität. Wissenschaftsgeschichtliche Studien zum deutschen Realismus: Keller, Raabe und Fontane. 1991.

Vol. 7 Karen Pawluk Danford : The Family in Adalbert Stifter's Moral and Aesthetic Universe. A Rarefied Vision. 1991.

Vol. 6 Deborah S. Lund: Ambiguity as Narrative Strategy in the Prose Work of C.F. Meyer. 1990.

Vol. 5 Carl Steiner: Karl Emil Franzos, 1848–1904. Emancipator and Assimilationist. 1990.

Vol. 4 George F. Peters: "Der Große Heide Nr. 2". Heinrich Heine and the Levels of His Goethe Reception. 1989.

Vol. 3 Jeffrey L. Sammons: Imagination and History. Selected Papers on Nineteenth-Century German Literature. 1988.

Vol. 2 Alphonso A. Frost Jr.: Ernst Dronke: His Life and His Works. 1989.

Vol. 1 Ursula Franklin: Exiles and Ironists. Essays on the Kinship of Heine and Laforgue. 1988.

FSC
www.fsc.org
MIX
Papier | Fördert
gute Waldnutzung
FSC® C083411

Kolibri 360 GmbH
Ferdinand-Jühlke-Straße 7
99095 Erfurt, Deutschland
produktsicherheit@kolibri360.de